MetaAutomation

MetaAutomation

Quality Automation for Faster and More Trustworthy Software Development

By Matt Griscom

MetaAutomation © Copyright 2018 Matt Griscom

ISBN 978-0-9862704-2-0

Library of Congress Control Number: 2018909974

Printed in the United States of America

Cover design: Kate Basart/Union Pageworks

Note on cover design:

The Minkowski diagram shows an equivalence between space and time. For this book, it represents a broadening of perspective, analogous to the "Meta" of MetaAutomation. See the section "The Need for a Pattern Language" on pages 70-71 for more information.

Dedication

I dedicate this book to my wife Suzanne for her patience and support — and for being my muse.

Brief Contents

List of Figures

Table of Contents

Foreword by Michael Corning

Today, it is all too common to see a test team test the wrong thing in the wrong way. Too much time is spent getting the test to the place in the code where the true value add for the product starts to work. Too often, tests produce unreliable results. The problem is that the quality of the product is often higher than the quality of the test. Matt's book measurably reduces the uncertainty that attends all uninformed, ad hoc, approaches to testing. Matt's MetaAutomation framework is the first step toward the ultimate goal of correcting this quality inversion.

Herbert Simon once said,

> *All correct reasoning is merely a grand scheme of tautology, but only God has direct access to that fact.*

In successful software development, "best practice" balances freedom of choice at each step of the work. In other words, of all the possible solutions to a problem, only one fits in the grand scheme. Moving from freedom of choice to best practice is not a subjective matter of opinion or style. Rather, a best practice is based on observation. It demonstrably and consistently produces superior results. This is not magic. It is learning. It is not learning about one thing; it is about learning how all the parts work together. This is the fundamental reason why constraints on design always produce better design. The designs are better because they are informed by more knowledge.

MetaAutomation asserts that if you build on its design patterns, the probability goes up that you ship a higher quality product in less time. Yes, there are other factors that influence the quality of a shipped product, but you will know that Matt is telling the truth and not just selling books if you give his method a good-faith effort. Simply put, it works because it is empirical.

Matt was a member of a diverse and select group of Software Design Engineers in Test at Microsoft that I formed to find new ways to more effectively test software. The central theme of this work was to discover design patterns, not for the product, but for the tests and test infrastructure. I used to say, "The uninspected test is not worth executing, and the un-designed test is not work inspecting." I only needed one member of this group to succeed to justify everyone's effort. Matt has emerged as that individual. My work here is done.

In the meantime, your work has just begun.

Thinking about design is never enough, though how design affects thought is always a good thing. Design is a verb. Matt shows you how to do it, and why it is the right thing to do right. As the chiasm says, "knowing how to build the right thing is not the same as knowing how to build the thing right." Matt's test design framework provides a much-needed service to the software development process: to borrow a powerful observation from George Gilder's latest book, *Knowledge and Power: The Information Theory of Capitalism and How it is Revolutionizing Our World*, Matt's framework is a "low entropy carrier" of a "high entropy signal." What this means for testers is that Matt's framework saves you hundreds of hours of wasted test development, execution, and investigation time by removing the entropy that distracts you, absent the framework. Put differently, words we use to describe the transition from a high entropy state to a low entropy state include learning, education, or knowledge. If your test development process has as much entropy as your product development process, it is less likely that you will produce a high-quality product. The odds are against you because the uncertainty of both states of uncertainty together must be higher than either state taken separately. The knowledge captured in Matt's "low entropy carrier" translates directly into better odds of successfully shipping a product that customers crave.

Matt's design framework is very pragmatic, and his book does not mention entropy at all. But from my reading, I can see how I can drop the kind of math and science I try to bring to software testing directly into his framework, substantially extending his framework's capabilities (and making my math and science more transparent and accessible to 21st century testing). This book is not just important for testers today, it is important for tomorrow, too.

One more thing: Matt is an excellent writer, and that is not very common in a world where most communication is from human to machine instead of human-to-human. Matt's descriptions are clear and direct. His code is well-designed, comprehensible, and extensible.

Michael Corning

Senior Data Scientist

Microsoft Skype

Foreword by Wayne Roseberry

MetaAutomation fills a gap that really needed filling. Testers, developers, and software engineers of various shape and form wrestle with automated tests, sometimes loving them, often cursing them, and most certainly frustrated by them. There have been many attempts at kits, and tools, and languages that were supposed to solve the testing automation problem. There has been in the first decade or so since the turn of the 21st century to re-awaken an emphasis on unit testing, a welcome turn of events that was birthed from necessity with the trends to ship fast and frequently. But with that shift came a backlash against end to end tests. Aren't tests that run the full application unreliable, slow, unstable, and expensive? And aren't they all just a pile of messy code? What good are they after all?

As so many product groups have found from the anti-integrated system test backlash, those end to end tests provide critical information. They check functionality that escapes the unit test. They check assumptions that only surface when the whole product is brought together.

But none of that changes an important point: most end to end tests were written without regard to the design patterns necessary to achieve rapidly delivered, reliably evaluated, and business relevant information about the product. Most end to end tests were written in environments where product cycles were long – month, years in the making. Most to end tests were born in a world where it was just assumed that eventually, somehow, a team of testers would manually dig through arcane and obscure test logs to isolate which failures were worthy of a developer's time and which were not. Take time to consider coding patterns for test automation? Nobody saw the point of it, or if they did, they certainly were not going to get anybody's attention making the case for it.

We do not live in the same world. We deliver product more often, more quickly. We listen more intimately and respond more quickly to customer needs. If one does not, their competitor does. That world cannot afford verifications that take weeks and months to finally land a bug on a developer's desk. To meet the needs of the modern software market, the discipline and the craft of test automation has to evolve.

Matt Griscom has built an answer to that next step. In some cases, formalizing movements and trends that are already happening in bits and pieces elsewhere, in other places applying pure invention, but in doing so producing a set of patterns (or pattern language – Matt is more formal about this than I tend to be) which make pragmatic and practical sense. I recommend MetaAutomation to anybody looking to put their thumb on the question "what is the right way to approach test automation?"

Wayne Roseberry

Principal Software Engineer

Microsoft

Preface

I live with a curse: I always look to the bigger picture when it helps understanding, and where I see big problems that I think have obvious solutions, I cannot let go... even if it consumes a part of me or gets me in bits of trouble sometimes. I am an idealist.

In the realm of functional software quality with automation, I see significant business value poured onto the floor and lost. Software projects going ahead with important quality questions deferred to a time when the business costs of encountering and addressing them are much higher, whether the cost is theoretical risk or realized. There is unseen opportunity cost of doing software quality with blinders on, and QA people doing things in ways that limit their value to the team. These things motivate me. We can do much better.

I also love the fussy techy details of software engineering that make the bigger picture possible. See the working samples of this book for concrete realizations of this.

It has been an adventure of discovery and elucidation.

In earlier career exploits, I have done things like earn two degrees in physics, implement DICOM Media[1] for a cross-platform project on the International Space Station, and do innovative and valuable work in the trenches of quality automation as precursors and fragments of the thesis of this book.

---

[1] I did this in C, in an extremely fussy grammar that supported inheritance and method overloading.

Why This Book

Current practices in quality automation are not capable of NOT dropping business value on the floor. This book shows how to fix that.

This book also shows how, given that information from driving and measuring the system under test (SUT) is all preserved in a robust format, the team can do powerful, wonderful, and valuable things with that information!

Ship software faster, at higher quality. Make big improvements to transparency, communication, cohesion, and collaboration on your team. Take down the silo walls between different job roles. Strengthen your support for positive software quality trends, like DevOps and Analytics.

Functional software quality is ripe for disruption, but people need very good reasons to embrace the change. This book gives those reasons. For software that matters the opportunity costs of the conventional approach are too great to ignore.

The thesis of MetaAutomation forms a coherent whole. It cannot nearly fit in a single blog post, or a paper, or even a series of blog posts or papers. It can only fit in a book with cross-references, references, and links. The book asks a lot of the reader, but I tried to make it easy as possible with many internal links as well as external ones, to pull together the many ideas and perspectives on what this means.

A very important thing about this book: it does not claim to solve all software quality problems, or even all behavioral software quality problems. But it does replace some practices with much better ones, and in integrates well with others.

I hope to show value to persuade software quality practitioners to move to a new gestalt[2] for the field that includes all information that has value to the business, works for the whole business, and, where possible, measures quality for the system as an end-user would experience it.

Whence This Book

This book is the result of my journey of many years through software quality practice, innovation, learning, teaching, research, blogging, and discovery, all driven by that idealistic passion.

3rd Edition

For the 3rd edition – this book – I broke out the Hierarchical Steps and Prioritized Requirements patterns for impact and clarity and did extensive work with The Hillside Group to improve the way I expressed the MetaAutomation pattern language. I filled out the quality automation problem space with a few other patterns, too.

---

[2] The organized whole, greater than the sum of the parts. Gestalt is a borrowed German word for shape or form and is used to describe human perception of the whole. The "whole" of this book is similar in concept to the quality automation problem space and the MetaAutomation pattern language that groups patterns to address it.

A third sample implementation makes the learning curve less steep.

Three paradigm shifts are more even and easier to remember than the six of the 2nd edition.

I left some unnecessary stuff out and improved the organization and the writing overall.

The research that went into the 3rd edition is much deeper than it was for the 2nd.

There are many other smaller improvements as well, plus one very big one: My friend Adrian Bourne worked with me to create many wonderful illustrations of visual metaphors to enrich the material and bind it together.

Gratitude

Depending on what or how you count, I have been working on this project for about 25 years, which virtually ensures that I will miss people who helped me along the way. I am grateful not only to those who have helped me in the five-year history of this book and earlier editions, but also to the many people whose insights have sharpened my own thinking. I am fortunate for the insight and guidance that appear on so many of the pages that follow.

Here are some of these people alphabetized by first name:

Alain Anyouzoa gave excellent (and positive) feedback on the MetaAutomation samples. I am grateful for his detailed reading which alerted me to many points I needed to clarify, and insights into how readers might approach the material.

Alan Page gave terrific feedback and at the perfect time. His reading was very thorough, and his feedback thoughtful and nimble, Socratic, supportive, and kind.

Alex Raizman did an extremely helpful code review for me of the sample project and reminded me of the inherent tension of an unusual amount of overhead for just one check. This prompted me to write something on that tension in the introduction to the sample in line with the code.

Bill Hodghead contributed some important, current perspectives on the uses of analytics as compared to synthetics and conventional automation, allowing me to improve the value of my book for those who use analytics, or plan to do so, in their quality measurements.

Brian Gaudreau offered his encouragement and a great sounding board for my work. He generously went out of his way to meet with me several times for interesting and stimulating discussions on what PNSQC was doing and how my work fit with the organization.

Christopher Preschern gave generous and detailed feedback on an early draft of the 3rd edition, and later on a more polished draft, showing me where I could make improvements to my pattern presentation and pointing out errors in the text that nobody else noticed.

Chris Struble proved how lucky I am to have so many people give feedback on my work, given that everybody learns differently and notices different things. Chris saw things that nobody else did and provided some excellent suggestions on improving the clarity of the work.

Colm Harrington has generously helped me at several stages during my discovery and writing process, from his busy job in the trenches of managing software quality. He found time in his schedule to give me detailed and actionable feedback on the second and third editions of the MetaAutomation book. In many places, he pointed me to points of confusion and missing details that I was no longer able to see because I was in the middle of it.

Dorothy Graham gave valuable feedback on testing types and many thoughtful discussions, including her challenge to me to clarify my perspective on Glenford Myers' mistake.

Douglas Hoffman took the time out of his terribly busy schedule to ask some very smart questions on my wording and show me what needed clarification. I am also grateful that he showed me many things that I was better off leaving out.

Elisabeth Hendrickson and I had some great conversations about software quality. She also gave me some great pointers on the business of software consulting and introduced me to some great thinkers in the business.

Gene Gotimer taught me some essential elements of DevOps, which enriched my picture of how MetaAutomation can integrate with the DevOps movement.

Gerard Meszaros encouraged me to work with The Hillside Group on patterns. He is an authority on the topic and gave some important pointers on creating and expressing patterns as part of a pattern language. He also gave me incredibly detailed feedback on more than one occasion. His writings on patterns gave guidance and inspiration.

Harvin Queen, with his great patience and ability for meticulous detail, gave helpful feedback on an early version of this book.

James Coplien helped by engaging me with stimulating discussions on essential properties of patterns in general.

Jamie Campbell gave feedback for testing types and the Hierarchical Steps pattern, and an incredibly detailed review of a 3rd edition draft with some excellent high-level comments as well. He and I also had many discussions of how data structure relates to the mission of his employer, Tableau Software.

Jeffrey Weston gave me valuable pointers and important encouragement. His concern that the Smart Retry pattern might lower the standard for robustness in automated tests inspired more discussion of the issue, and a strengthening of the pattern. His feedback for the Automated Triage pattern was especially helpful.

Joe Dillon runs Quardev, a Seattle testing and QA talent company. Quardev provides a very welcoming bi-monthly forum called QASIG for software quality professionals to gather and exchange innovative ideas about doing software better (with pizza and beer!). I thank Joe for offering this forum to help idea exchange in the community, and for me personally, help me nurture MetaAutomation from the first stages onward.

John Ruberto gave me a great deal of wonderful, detailed feedback, including useful thoughts on making it a better book.

Mark Tomlinson helped me with some supportive and encouraging discussions on performance, software quality, and thought leadership.

Michael Corning was an early booster of my work and gave an academically rigorous and valuable review. I learned from Michael the power of XML when smartly applied.

Michael John and I had a great discussion on my samples, in which he pushed me to make the timeouts data-driven in the artifacts in an easily accessible way.

Neil Harrison is deeply knowledgeable and experienced with patterns and pattern languages, and very quick and thorough with his feedback and support.

Patrick McMonagle reviewed my original book on MetaAutomation and gave great feedback.

Paul Gerrard found time in his busy schedule to review the important introductory chapters. I like the way Paul thinks and very much appreciate his willingness to listen, learn, and seek out a better way. We had many thoughtful, interesting, and useful discussions.

Paul Grizzaffi helped with his deep perspective on code comments.

Rebecca Wirfs-Brock helped with discovery of the Event-Driven Check pattern.

Richard (Dick) Gabriel organized and ran writers' workshops on patterns and pattern languages and was important to sustaining that community of structured ideas and communication. Dick gave me excellent feedback on my own writings on MetaAutomation.

Robert Biddle gave great feedback on my paper for PLoP 2017 and helped me interface with academia.

Robin Goldsmith gave the expertise and help I really needed for my sections on the importance of requirements and how they work, through his excellent book on the topic.

Seth Eliot offered many valuable insights into how professionals in the field might receive the details of MetaAutomation, leading to some great clarifications and filling out of some descriptions. He also gave helpful suggestions on formatting a highly technical book such as this.

Thomas Mercer walked me through preflight on a Cessna 172 and helped me find documentation to present an example on this for the Hierarchical Steps pattern.

Wayne Roseberry provided inspiration through his innovative work on quality with Microsoft Office products. He worked with me through many thoughtful and generative discussions on the problems and solutions faced by the Office team at Microsoft and gave a foreword as well to the 3rd edition. Wayne gave me wonderful and actionable feedback for my testing types classification and the Hierarchical Steps pattern.

I also contributed to and worked with some groups and gatherings, so here they are in rough chronological order:

Preparing for my presentation at PNSQC[3] 2014, Randy King and Karyn Zerr reviewed my paper that led to the Atomic Check pattern. They both showed a terrific eye for structure and detail, and gave good, constructive, and useful criticism.

On my paper for PLoP[4] 2016 introducing the Hierarchical Steps pattern, Rebecca

Wirfs-Brock shepherded my work and gave great feedback. At the conference, I workshopped the paper with Shererazade Benzerga, Michael John, Clif Kussmaul, and of course Rebecca. Through the workshop process they gave detailed and actionable constructive criticism.

In addition to his individual feedback on my book, Chris Preschern shepherded my paper on MetaAutomation in preparing for VikingPLoP 2017. At the conference, it was workshopped by Malte Brunnlieb, Veli-Pekka Eloranta, Takashi Iba, Klaus Marquardt, Ville Reijonen, Andreas Rüping, Michael Weiss, Joe Yoder, and me. Thank you, gentlemen!

Neil Harrison shepherded my (too long) paper on MetaAutomation with excellent and insightful feedback in preparing for PLoP 2017. At the conference, Robert Biddle, Lisa Hvatum, Tayyaba Nafees, Rebecca Wirfs-Brock, and Tim Yao all workshopped the paper, which resulted in powerful feedback.

As a volunteer for PNSQC 2018, Dave Patterson gave useful and actionable feedback on my paper on why "Test Automation" is broken.[5]

An important part of my discovery process involved speaking about it. I will always be grateful to the members of Wallingford Toastmasters of Seattle Washington for helping me improve and clarify my messaging; there is nothing like peer

---

[3] The Pacific Northwest Software Quality Conference

[4] Pattern Languages of Programs is a series of conferences sponsored by The Hillside Group.

[5] That point appears in this book as Chapter 3.

evaluations in a constructive, safe environment. Speaking practice helps to condense and improve the material.

I also worked with some great professionals along the way, presented here in rough chronological order:

Rebecca Osman and Erin McGonaugh of Seattle are excellent speech coaches that helped me fine-tune my communications craft.

Career coach Ashley Guberman has a wonderful ability to look at things from important, creative, yet unconventional perspectives. She skillfully found and challenged my assumptions; her global thinking lifted me out of a deep technical focus on my topic just when that was what I needed.

Management consultant Johanna Rothman introduced me to impact mapping and gave me great feedback on how to make mine work better.

Adrian Bourne is both a good friend and wonderful artist and a pleasure to work with! I gave him visual metaphors and scenarios with just enough detail, and with wonderful creativity he filled in details to make powerful images.

Jill Rothenberg was my editor. She applied her fresh, professional literary talent to create many suggestions for improvements, including literary grace well beyond my capabilities and saw issues that I simply became blind to after a while.

Linda Carlson gave wonderful guidance on a variety of topics around formatting, presenting, publishing, and promoting the book.

Kate Basart, thank you for designing beautiful covers for my books, and for being a pleasure to work with.

The greatest debts of gratitude go to my family:

I thank my late mother, Joanne Starr Griscom, for pushing me to have courage in my convictions.

I thank my father Dr. Nathan Thorne Griscom for many helpful comments, his great editorial skill, and his confidence that I would go far.

My lovely wife Suzanne provided me with wonderful editorial feedback and suggestions in amplifying the concepts of the book, thoughts on the requirements of each section, and the emotional support over years of work to keep going!

Section 1

Introduction to MetaAutomation

Chapter 1
The Big-Picture Executive Summary

As Albert Einstein wrote,

> *We cannot solve our problems with the same thinking we used when we created them.*

Software quality is getting more important every year.

To fix the broken "test automation," to make higher-quality software and do it faster, we must think anew on the value of quality practices to the software business *and* how to maximize that value.

This Book

The focus of this book is using automation for quality to get very fast, detailed, actionable feedback on software behavior and its performance communicated around the team, to enable developing and shipping that software faster.

Without making any big changes to how your team might currently approach doing quality with automation, this book has many good ideas to help that effort and many prompts to rethink the "how" or the "why" of what is best.

The big step — the quantum leap! — that this book asks of your team is to see the business value in recording *all* that your software does when driven by automation, and then to make it happen. With this information, the tools I give you can empower the whole team to ship software faster and at higher quality. The most powerful techniques presented in this book are impossible without that information.

Before this book, there was no way to record most of it.[6]

Quality Automation

The quality automation problem space is the scope of opportunities to automate measuring, recording, and delivering quality information on the system under test (SUT) to the people and processes of the software business.

This book shows how to record and present to the business in great and trustworthy detail, faster than possible before:

- What is working
- How fast each interaction with the system delivers
- What is not working

And, it enables the business to

- Fix bugs more quickly than before
- Protect the team from churn

Plus, support in unprecedented and trustworthy detail

- Find the precise measured quality risk
- Describe quality trends over time

Quality automation is the automation to create preconditions, drive the SUT, make measurements, make "smart" informed choices about getting a second or third opinion on a result, collate, send the data to specific people and processes as needed, and present the quality data in role-appropriate ways to all people in the business who care about quality.

Quality automation by itself does nothing to change SUT quality, but it delivers exactly what is needed to developers and others to make fast and informed quality-related decisions.

MetaAutomation

The quality automation problem space divides naturally into distinct problems with distinct solutions. Each solution — for example, how to drive the SUT, how to record the information, how to determine to whom notifications should go, etc. — corresponds to current behaviors of how people solve that problem today. The patterns fit together with easily-defined dependencies, and as a set they fill the quality automation problem space to form a pattern language. This pattern language is what I call "MetaAutomation."

The "meta" of MetaAutomation refers to the more abstract, higher-level view; more than just considering automation as using machines (or, computers and information processing) to replicate what people already do manually or by cobbling existing tools together, I consider the ideal solution that automation can offer to the quality automation problem space *without* being limited by pre-existing practices and ideas.

---

[6] The first and second editions of the MetaAutomation book go into this as well, but this third edition does a better job of it.

The MetaAutomation pattern language forms an introduction to the quality automation problem space *and* it describes a platform-independent and language-independent implementation of that space.

Why do I use a language of patterns to discover, describe, and communicate these concepts? Because the tradition of patterns, started by architect Christopher Alexander in the 1970s, is the most appropriate and effective tool I can apply towards helping teams develop higher-quality software, faster.

Figure 16 on page 73 shows a "pattern map" to MetaAutomation.

Value to You

This book shows how the team can ship software faster, at higher quality *and* higher confidence in that quality.

This book gives you, the software executive, an unprecedented best practice that your team can offer for visibility into the workings of your software system. The beauty of the approach offered here is that the visibility it offers you is part of the same approach that gives your team the ability to achieve vastly better communication and collaboration around what your software system is doing (or, not doing).

This book gives you, the software quality professional, the big picture of the business value you can achieve with quality automation, and how you can produce far more of that value for the team than with conventional practices. It puts you at the center of the larger team for communications and collaboration across geographies and across all roles concerned with SUT behavior and performance.

This book gives you, the software developer, a means to develop software that matters *faster* and *at lower risk* with better clarity, transparency, and communication between teams and geographies.

Unifying Software Development with Quality

In the last ten years or so, quality automation and software development have been reducing the time lag and the communications barrier that separates them through what is sometimes known as the "shift left" movement. Some of this process of bringing the team closer together depends on the trust that developers have in the QA role and their automation. It also depends on the recognition across the larger team that there is an important function in verifying that the software system, after a given change, still does what the business needs it to do. Otherwise, the quality role is limited to bug-seeker.

> *If you focus on finding bugs, the developers will treat you like servants. (Gerrard 2016b)*

To strengthen the software development process, the team must bring these two roles closer together in a way that helps them both.

> *A balanced perspective cannot be acquired by studying disciplines in*

pieces but through pursuit of the consilience among them. Such unification will come hard. But I think it is inevitable. (Wilson 1998)

By the same quantum leap I mentioned earlier — recording *all* that your software does when driven by automation — MetaAutomation brings development and quality much closer together. Through new speed, focus, and detail in what the automation measures and communicates, it also brings the broader team closer. This enables shipping higher-quality software, faster.

Occam's Razor

In the 14th century, the English Franciscan friar William of Ockham gave us what is known as "Occam's razor" or the "law of parsimony:" given competing ways of understanding, the one with fewest assumptions is best.

For example, in 19th century England, Charles Darwin showed that to understand the riotous diversity of life, there is no need to assume a god.

In early 20th century Germany, Albert Einstein showed that to understand light, space, and time, there is no need to assume an "ether" of space.

With this book I show when applying automation to measure, record, and communicate functional behavior and performance, there is no need to be

constrained by — in fact, we are better off not considering — manual testing efforts, e.g., in the test cases or how we arrange verifications. We are then free to consider what works best for the team with automation. Even better, we can help the manual test role in ways that conventional "test automation" cannot.

I also show that we are better off without the assumption that good automation code must look just like product code. Again, we are free to consider what works best for the team with automation.

It is also important to note, however, that while good manual testing practice needs paying close attention to interactions with the SUT, conventional practices for "test automation" are very poor at recording interactions.[7] This book shows how to vastly improve how the automation records and persists interactions with the system. This enables the quality automation to help the always-important manual testing role, which is much more effective (and makes better business sense) than the other way around.

Knowledge is Power

Sir Francis Bacon, Thomas Jefferson, and others made this point:

Knowledge is power.

The sad truth is that today, when automation drives the SUT, it drops nearly all the knowledge of SUT behavior on the

---

[7] This is also a weakness of automation with BDD. See section "Behavioral driven development (BDD)" on pages 34-35.

floor. When the team does this for quality purposes, i.e., with what is known as "test automation," the dropped information is potentially very valuable. People doing manual testing on a product know this well, so they keep their eyes and other senses open and even use tools to record more data as desired. Yet with conventional automation, the information is dropped. The loss of this knowledge causes risk when quality issues are unobserved or cannot be efficiently communicated outside the QA team. There is direct business cost when QA people must take the time to reproduce a problem (or, try to; success in reproducing a problem is not assured) and debug through automation to regain — temporarily — the information that was lost.

This book describes the nature and causes of this costly practice, shows an elegant solution that preserves the knowledge — and the *structure* of the knowledge — and makes it easily available across the larger team.

Knowledge preservation, structure, and communication to add value: these are the basic values MetaAutomation offers. Tribal knowledge is less important when quality automation driving the SUT behavior is self-documenting in a form that is readily accessible to all roles on the team.

More value follows, including other solutions to minimize quality risk while maximizing speed and communication effectiveness.

Maslow's Hammer

Beware the cognitive bias described by Abraham Maslow

> *I suppose it is tempting, if the only tool you have is a hammer, to treat everything as if it were a nail. (Maslow 1968)*

MetaAutomation is a powerful concept for getting the fastest, most trustworthy, and complete answer to the question "Does the system do what we need it to do?" as well as many other benefits described in this book. It obsoletes some software quality practices, but not all of them. You need other tools and techniques as well, including ones that are well known in the field. See the section "Benefits for quality practices" on pages 28-35 for more discussion of this.

Looking to the Big Picture

If "small picture" is the traditional scattered use of simple log statement events to get information back from automation code — and only caring about results in case of check[8] failure — the big picture is persisting *all* the procedure information in a way that logs cannot: applying the Hierarchical Steps pattern described on pages 85-98 as part of the Atomic Check implementation described on pages 99-119.

---

[8] Check is a type of Test procedure that is specific to automation, where verifications are determined in the code that drives the automation and human powers of observation do not apply. Check is further defined in the glossary on page 219.

A similar transition is moving from sole emphasis on the pass-fail of an automated procedure to detailed, trustworthy, and complete information on how automation drives and measures the SUT, in a format that elegantly captures procedure context and supports rich and robust communication around the larger team.

Traditionally, the small picture "Test Automation" gives value just to the test or QA role.[9] The "automation" is to blithely automate what they would do manually (with resulting quality risk – see pages 11-22). Value to the team outside QA is like the value in case of all the tests being run manually; they still must be reported somehow, and it is up to the test or QA role to do the reporting.

In the big picture, the quality automation problem space describes quality management value across the whole team, not just QA. Automation does more than just measure the product with automated checking; it also creates detailed, deep, and trustworthy knowledge of what the product does and how fast it does it and communicates that knowledge across the whole team. There is enough information now that automation can also solve the flaky test problem (as with the Smart Retry pattern on pages 141-150) and send directed notifications as needed (as with the Automated Triage pattern on pages 151-154). Automation delivers the quality information across the larger team in a format that is useful for all roles.

In the small picture of traditional "test automation," the procedures are based on a manual test. In the big picture, the automated procedure is based on the ideal for measuring and creating knowledge with automation. A recipe for creating that ideal is described as part of the Atomic Check pattern (pages 99-119).

Small picture software development puts a big emphasis on unit testing but defers the big picture that includes all dependencies — which, these days, means the internet or a constellation of devices — until later. The big picture of MetaAutomation makes limited use of unit tests[10] and tests all dependencies as early as possible, even making it possible to do so before a check-in commits to the code repository. Meaningful quality measurements therefore come much earlier, which reduces quality risk.

---

[9] With teams that use combined engineering, this could include developers who are running and analyzing automation on the SUT.

[10] Unit tests are worthwhile when they relate to SUT requirements. See Appendix 4 on Unit Tests for more information (pages 203-204).

Chapter 2
Book Layout

Overview

The Introduction is long because there is much about conventional practices to reconsider. There are many chances here for the reader to open her eyes to opportunity costs in the business. There may be parts in the section "The Value of This Book" (pages 22-35) to skip over because they do not apply to everybody; readers who do read this whole section might find it repetitive.

The section on the three paradigm shifts tries to show the value and the inevitability of looking at some things in new ways: the ways needed to fully benefit from this book.

The pattern language MetaAutomation is a guide to thinking about, talking about, and implementing your quality automation solution. If any part of either the Hierarchical Steps pattern or the Atomic Check pattern seems confusing, please jump to the samples and try them out, or get engaged as described in the "Future Patterns" section on pages 159-160.

The Sample Solutions (pages 161-176) show a way of implementing Hierarchical Steps within the Atomic Check pattern, plus they show some *very* cool and useful stuff like performance information at every node and how to run a single check across multiple tiers with one coherent structure for a check result.

The section "Overview of Business-Facing Quality Automation" shows how the team might implement some of the business-facing concepts for the quality automation problem space, and how they might appear to people in the business.[11]

The Dance

Think of this book as a dance. By picking up this book, you have chosen to engage with a very new and empowering view of the quality automation space. But one reading might not make it all clear. I hope the many page references to items in the book will help join the different concepts together.

By "very new," I mean that it is much more than your usual proportion of innovative ideas compared to a grounding of established ones. This is not the book where you are likely to think "Yes, good, I know that part already, and I'm ready to move on to the 10% of the book that is new material."

If this book seems repetitive in parts, that is good: you are recognizing the repetitive part of the dance. A dance is a pattern and patterns repeat. Go back to sections that did not make sense before and use the references as needed.

Please remember that I encourage feedback, especially if it tries to be constructive or oriented towards resolution.[12] Get involved, ask questions, suggest improvements, or explain when something really is not clear or needs to be improved. Good, useful input will be credited and acknowledged in future work.

In the long term, filling out and defining the quality automation problem space, and either MetaAutomation or something that supersedes it, will be a community effort.

Code Samples

There is no code in this book, but working solutions to build, run, modify, and play around with, or port to another language or any platform are available on GitHub and linked from the MetaAutomation.net web site. They are discussed in the Sample Solutions section (pages 161-176).

Working solutions are a better and more meaningful context for the code, as compared to inline in a book.

Review Questions Supplement the Material

Each major section has review questions at the end. The review questions, with answers at the end of the book, give another perspective on the material. They are also there to remind readers of important points in the preceding section.

The Glossary is Your Friend

The glossary on pages 217-225 defines terms that are new with this book or might need clarification for the context of this book. I avoid conflict with general usages where possible. The meaning for any one term used for this book might be a subset of meanings in a more general context.

---

[11] See also "Overview of Business-Facing Quality Automation" on pages 179-192.

[12] See "Future Patterns for MetaAutomation" on pages 159-160 for information on getting involved.

Chapter 3
Fixing "Test Automation"

People tend to limit their options and reinforce counterproductive habits with the phrase "test automation." This section describes why even using the phrase is limiting people and what to do about it.

A basic concept for this book is that quality automation has very different capabilities than people doing manual testing, whether the people use tools or not. Figure 1 on page 12 introduces the visual metaphor of the automation robot recording structured data on a data ball, as part of the quality automation problem space. This book has robots doing various things, all representing what automation can do for quality.

Clarity in the Quality Context
This is not industrial automation
Automating for quality is not like industrial automation, or even flight deck automation for pilots. Those types of automation are for production; they automate what a person might do, or even what a person is

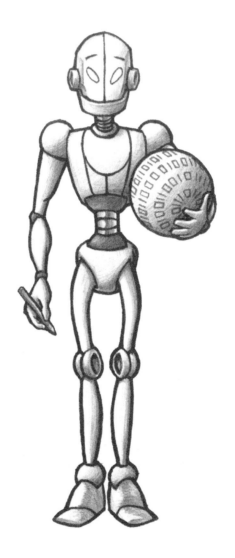

Fig. 1. The quality automation metaphor: robot recording a databall.

incapable of doing without tools, to deliver value. Ideally, they do it faster, better, and cheaper than what a human could do. The result could be more cars manufactured, or a safer, smoother flight across the Atlantic Ocean.

Automation for quality is about making measurements, creating useful information, making a Boolean decision— does a failure condition exist? — and communicating the result.

Understanding manual test

Manual testing is testing done by humans. People lead it, either following scripts ("scripted" testing) or hunches or guidance about general areas of functionality ("exploratory" testing). People see and experience the SUT, and do detective work, and note if some quality aspect is (potentially) actionable. If it is, the person enters a bug.

If the person testing the SUT uses a tool, e.g. generated data, a web client that calls an SUT API, or a network sniffer, it is still manual test because it is the *person* who collects the observations and decides whether an issue around the SUT is actionable or not.

People are smart, and manual testing is very open-ended and creative. Everybody on the team who interacts with the SUT is engaging in manual testing, because anyone on the team might notice something — or understand something — that others do not. Whether or not people apply a tool towards this end (besides the SUT itself), they collect observations and create the knowledge.

If an automated procedure runs N times, and succeeds every time with performance data, a manual review of the data to see if performance or consistency is acceptable, is a kind of manual test — even if such a review could easily be automated.

The need for manual testing will always be part of the software development process.

Quality automation

Automation for quality is not about production. Code for such automation never affects customers directly.[13]

Quality automation runs, by default, without human interaction. It supports functional and performance quality for the SUT, and push- and pull-communication around the team.[14] It does not change SUT quality directly; it supports the software business' need for information about functional and performance quality.

The Broken Name

"Automation" applied to "Test"

In ancient times – ancient, by the software perspective – "test" was the best word to apply to measuring software quality. People did "test."

Then, people applied automation — scripting to automatically drive the SUT etc. — to do some of this work, faster and cheaper. It was simple and obvious to put these two words together: "Test Automation" was born.

---

[13] This assumes that the automation is well written and isolated, which becomes especially important for testing in production (TIP).

[14] Push communication could be emails or other notifications sent to team members who need to know. Pull communication could be query and analysis done on a quality portal intranet site.

To a limited extent, it realized the promise of "test automation," too. Despite some challenges, for example as Alan Page said

> *Making good end-to-end GUI tests is one of the hardest tasks in programming. (Page 2018)*

it really does do some measurements faster and cheaper than people could.

If it were possible to use automation to replicate all that a human tester can do, but faster and cheaper, then that would be perfect. But, it just *is not so*; not even close.

A human can be very good at manual test, typically over a complete end-to-end scenario. On the other hand, a computer brings more value faster with a simple procedure to do the fast, repeatable automation that this book is about.

As Isaac Asimov wrote,

> *The human specialty … is the ability to see problems as a whole, to grasp solutions through intuition or insight; to see new combinations; to be able to make extraordinarily perceptive and creative guesses.*

By contrast,

> *Computers … are extraordinarily good in some ways. They possess capacious memories, have virtually instant and unfailing recall, and demonstrate the ability to carry through vast numbers of repetitive arithmetical operations without weariness or error. (Asimov, 1986)*

The value a human tester brings is very different from the value that automation for quality brings. Both have strong and weak points. That is an important basis for this book. Understanding what quality automation can do well, and using that understanding, can vastly increase the business value of automation for quality.

Mostly, "test automation" is an oxymoron, like "jumbo shrimp," "creation science," or "working vacation." It is a historical accident.

Linguistic relativity

The words we use influence how we think. That is Linguistic Relativity.[15] Teachers, politicians, and other professional communicators know this well.

The semantics of "test automation" tend to mislead people in the field. If a team has dedicated testers, the implication is that "automating" those tests means that the team can reduce costs by letting all those people go; the "test" value is all "automated," so we have the same quality value as before, but faster and cheaper… right? Managers are watching costs to the business, and they tend to accept the invitation — misleading in this case — to drastically reduce headcount. See the section "The manual testing role" on pages 55-56 for more on how MetaAutomation

---

[15] This is also known as the Sapir-Whorf hypothesis because researchers Edward Sapir and Benjamin Lee Whorf worked to support it, even though the two men never collaborated.

can make manual testing more fun and productive.

Fig. 2. Repeated procedures of automation are very poor at finding bugs.

People develop most tests manually, and many of these tests get "automated." Many tests that are automated, people also run manually at some point. "Test automation" implies that the design values for these tests is just the same, whether it runs manually or automated. But, that is not actually true. With an informed approach, we can do repeatable automation much better.

The "test automation" implication that the automation value-add is a simple amplification of the test role is misleading. In practice, that is how it has been used and is still used today, so quality data on the SUT must be reported to people outside the test or QA role with emails or an information radiator screen.[16] This superficially appears to the team to be just the same as if all the test were done manually, but faster. The opportunity cost of limiting the team to this kind of thinking is that the potential benefits of working with much better data on SUT behavior are unrealized. Improving the quality systems for the larger team – to ship software faster and at higher quality – is not on the radar, because with conventional practices, nobody knows how to do it; it looks impossible.

The Tyranny of Bugs

Testers who like books may have a copy of Glenford Myers' "The Art of Software Testing" from 1979. Myers wrote

> *Testing is the process of executing a program with the intent of finding errors. (Myers 1979, p. 5)*

He has much more to say on the topic as well, including this on the next page:

> *… since a test case that does not find an error is largely a waste of time and money… (Myers 1979, p. 6)*

Myers was clear and emphatic: if not finding bugs, you are wasting the team's time and money.

Of course, this was 1979, and software was vastly simpler back then *and* much less impactful on people's lives. I suspect that, through incorrect but well-intentioned reasoning, Myers arrived at an idea that was approximately correct at the time: looking for bugs, for as long as bugs continue to be found, was enough.

Myers' book was important for the community at the time, and very influential. Today, on a web search for exact text on the above quoted sentence, one can find a huge number of references.[17] The idea is still a significant meme!

It is an attractive idea, too, as an easy metric when measuring team member productivity: "How many bugs did you find today?"

---

[16] This could be, e.g., a large monitor on the office wall that shows basic quality status information for the product.

[17] From a search on February 27th, 2018, I get 3,610,000 results from Bing, 10,700 results from Google.

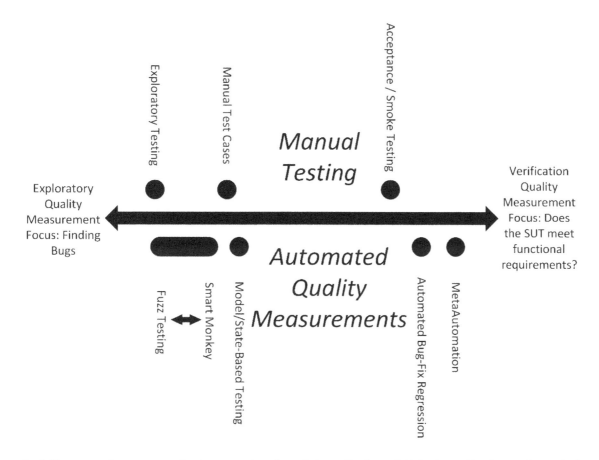

Fig. 3. The contrast between manual and automated quality techniques. The focus of this book puts MetaAutomation on the far right, but techniques of some sections add value for any automation driving the SUT for quality.

If "test" is all about finding bugs, then "test automation" must do the same, but faster... right?[18] Of course, repeatable automation can find and regress very significant bugs, but as a means of finding bugs, it is not very effective. Figure 3 above shows this in some detail; Figure 2 on page 15 shows this metaphorically. "Test automation" could get inappropriately devalued by leaders who do not know

better, when they discover it is very poor at finding bugs.[19]

In the same short-sighted way, leaders could devalue data from the SUT as well. If it does not find bugs, according to Myers, we do not care. By this thinking,

---

[18] I have heard a test manager ask for exactly that.

[19] Repeatable automation is poor at finding bugs at runtime in the lab or cloud. However, I have

found many bugs during development of automation to drive the SUT.

nobody minds dropping SUT data on the floor.[20]

The Cost of Missing Data

The missing SUT data means that, on failure of a bit of SUT-driving automation, it might be necessary for somebody on the automation team or QA role to reproduce the error (if possible) and debug through the automation at least once. Until that happens, the failure is not actionable. Most such failures are due to something that the QA role must fix (from my long experience doing this). This means that the failure might remain extant for many hours, so the team is hit by the significant cost of the task context-switch, and the time to follow up on the failure, *and* low trust in the automation that the QA team worked so hard to create.

As Huizinga and Kolowa wrote

> ... *if there is a problem with the code, it is best to uncover that problem as soon as it is introduced, when it is easiest, fastest, and least costly to fix it. (Huizinga and Kolowa 2007, p. 240)*

The first paradigm shift (pages 39-50) addresses preserving the data, and MetaAutomation shows how this means that a problem with the code can be made actionable for a team member, much more quickly than with the conventional approach.

For the complex and inter-connected software that people develop today, looking for bugs is important, but that alone is not good enough. To manage quality risk and keep the team moving forward, automation must give detailed and trustworthy answers to the question "Does the system do what we need it to do?" fast, reliably, and repeatedly.

The Missing Potential

The risks of automating manual tests

Tests designed as manual tests tend to be long and complicated, with many steps and many verifications. This is efficient for manual testing, especially if they lead through end-to-end scenarios. People running through these tests are smart, creative, flexible, and resourceful; they will find a way to complete a step even if a failure blocks the usual path. They will also find a way to make a measurement even if they must be creative about getting the information.

It is a common pattern to design procedures as manual tests, and then automate them.[21] But the results are usually not optimal quality automation:

---

[20] Or, letting the garbage collection process clean it up, system recover heap memory, or drop it off the stack etc.

[21] The person doing this work does not think of them as explicitly manual tests, but the person runs the test case manually first and since a manual interface is the context for any design decisions about the procedure, it is designed, by default, as manual.

- Given a long and complicated sequence of steps and measurements, an automated check would have many potential points of failure. Premature failure in the check causes blocked quality measurements and resulting quality risk.

- As a manual test, people do the procedure most often through a GUI. Automating a GUI tends to be slow and flaky, and in case of failure, the tester gets poor visibility into root cause. For quality aspects below the GUI layer, automating closer to the measured functionality — bottom-up testing — is faster and much more effective. See more on bottom-up testing on pages 64-65.

- People running manual tests may have multiple choices of how they interact with the product. They could drop that menu, for example, or push this button, to get the same response from the SUT. Automation might choose one or the other, or a different means of driving the SUT that works better for the automation.[22] The result might be a mismatch between what the automation does and what the team understands it to do.[23]

- People are smart, creative, and observant, and they are very good at finding and characterizing defects. Automation done well can be extremely powerful, as shown in this book, but it cannot see all that a human can (and is better off not trying, due to inefficiency and brittleness that would result from the attempt). Quality risk comes from misunderstanding about what a test case means for quality when run by a person, vs. what the "automated" version of that test case means for quality.

Quality automation has capabilities that manual test does not

The quality automation discussed in this book concerns driving and measuring the SUT, recording detailed results, and communicating them in a deeply useful way to all team members concerned with quality. This book focuses on the repeatable checks that the team needs to answer the question "Does the system do what we need it to do?" quickly, but some techniques here apply equally well to strengthen non-repeatable automation. For example, the Hierarchical Steps pattern (implemented as in the linked samples) is perfect for documenting what the SUT is driven to do for machine learning or model-based testing.

---

[22] A single repeatable check must do only one or the other, and the same every time.

[23] The Hierarchical Steps and Atomic Check patterns work together to solve the mismatch problem in a way not previously possible.

Repeatable quality automation offers these values that manual test cannot:

- Speed
- Reliability
- Repeatability
- Run cheaply at all hours, or in the lab or cloud
- Automated structured artifacts foster communication around the team on SUT behavior and quality

From the Association for Computing Machinery (ACM) draft Code of Ethics:

> *A computing professional should be transparent and provide full disclosure of all pertinent system limitations and potential problems. ... High quality professional work in computing depends on professional review at all stages. (ACM 2018)*

To help with this transparency, quality automation as envisioned with MetaAutomation provides transparency into SUT behavior and performance in much greater detail than is possible with either manual test or established practices of "test automation."

This enables a solution to the problem of false-positives or "flaky tests." The problem of defect escapes, where "we thought we tested that!" can be solved as well.[24] Detailed performance data comes for free.[25]

Manual test productivity is up because manual testers can use an intranet site to see exactly what was already verified with automation, and they can concentrate more on the exploratory testing they enjoy rather than the boring and repetitive running of test scripts.[26]

Sarbanes-Oxley

The Sarbanes-Oxley Act of 2002 (aka SOX) became law in the wake of the Enron scandal (Wikipedia, "Sarbanes-Oxley Act"). It concerns company financials, especially clarity and reliability of reporting. It is specific to the United States, but other countries have emulated it as well.

Section 302 of SOX includes requirements for timeliness, accuracy, and completeness of internal communications at a company about assets and operations. Section 404 focuses on risk assessment and disclosure of the effectiveness of a company's internal controls.

For a software company, MetaAutomation creates very strong stories for communication and risk management through:

- Complete, detailed, and correct assessments of software product quality, focused on business requirements of the system (and, regressions of fixed bugs)
- Actionable quality events around regressions, found and delivered

---

[24] See Hierarchical Steps on pages 85-98 and Atomic Check on pages 99-119.

[25] Every step in the hierarchy that passed or failed includes millisecond count in the artifact.

[26] See Queryable Quality on pages 155-158.

fast enough to prevent or quickly fix failures found by the quality automation

- A very detailed, searchable, and presentable record of software quality that uniformly spans time and all the business behaviors of the product that are accessible to quality automation

A 2009 paper in the International Journal of Business Governance and Ethics notes:

The overall regression results are consistent with the view that SOX has a favourable long-term favourable impact.[27] (Switzer and Lin 2009)

Whether or not your company is pursuing SOX compliance currently, MetaAutomation gives a very strong foundation of clarity and certainty about the quality and behavior of software under development or maintenance.

Less uncertainty means less risk. Higher visibility all around makes more efficient collaboration and happier teams.

Working software samples

The samples described on pages 161-176 show these features in working, modifiable code:

- Performance info at every step
- Data-driven configurable timeouts, at every step

- Checks mark failed steps from the failed leaf step up to the root of the hierarchy
- Checks mark blocked steps automatically
- During run of a multi-tiered check, each tier generates a hierarchy and the check combines them into the larger hierarchy for the check result[28]

Graduating to Quality Automation

For most of this book, I avoid the phrase "test automation." I do not even grandfather it in; other than lingual inertia, there is no reason to do so, even if existing practices never changed. It had well-meaning origins, but today it amounts to a historical accident, just like Myers' exclusive focus on bugs.[29] We who practice software quality with automation are better off without it.

I use the phrase "quality automation" instead, which opens the door to faster development, higher quality, better communication, collaboration, transparency and agility, and happier teams.

Best of all for the team, all the above value flows from the QA role, so the QA role becomes both a linchpin and a hero of product development.

---

[27] The repetition of "favourable" is in the original statement.
[28] The multi-tiered check is shown with Sample 3 on pages 173-176.

[29] This is detailed in "The Tyranny of Bugs" on pages 16-18.

In the conventional way of doing things, as Robin Goldsmith said

> *QA is often seen as an obstacle to progress! (Goldsmith 2016)*

This has been my experience, too. For example, in the fall of 2015, at the STARWEST conference in Anaheim, California, in a hall outside the meeting rooms, I overheard these words from a frustrated QA manager speaking into his phone:

> *I want to know why the QA team wasn't represented in the go-no-go meeting this morning!*

Jana Gierloff said in her presentation at STPCon of Spring 2017,

> *QA is responsible for assisting the whole team in providing high quality. (Gierloff 2017)*

MetaAutomation is a way of modeling and solving the quality automation problem space in an ideal way, to meet Gierloff's challenge as never before possible.

With MetaAutomation, quality is no longer a second-class citizen. The leaders in quality become the team heroes. QA gives the broader team unprecedented clarity into SUT behavior and performance, and with unprecedented timeliness as well.

The Value of This Book

This section discusses how MetaAutomation might affect distinct roles, team structures, software development methods, and quality

practices. Books in the field with less radical theses do not need to do this, but the changes described here have far-reaching implications. Please read where it applies to you, your team, or your interest.

MetaAutomation does not stand alone as a quality practice; other quality practices still supplement what this book can do, while not replacing it.

Ken Koster describes this in the abstract to his 2007 paper:

> *Compared to using a single quality technique, a diversified portfolio of techniques will typically be more effective and less variable. (Koster 2007)*

The section "Benefits for quality practices" on pages 28-35 briefly describes other quality practices and how they relate to MetaAutomation. The Hierarchical Steps pattern, and some aspects of the Atomic Check pattern, can help with existing automated and tool-assisted approaches to quality that are not the focus of this book.

Benefits for target audiences

Software teams

Faster feedback

MetaAutomation shows how to do quality automation *optimized* for what quality automation does well. This means feedback to answer the question "Does the system do what we need it to do?" faster and with more scalability than before.

This book focuses mostly on deterministic checks that do the same test with the SUT every time they are run, but techniques here are also very useful with non-deterministic checks including monkey testing or "big" testing.

Low false negative rate

False negatives happen when a check or set of checks pass to make the software look good, but in reality, there is a problem that automation failed to detect. These are related to defect escapes, where the defect is "escaped" because an end-user or customer runs into it before the team even knows about it. If the false negative is a surprise to the team, as in "I thought we tested that and found that it worked correctly," it might be due to a misunderstanding of what the team has tested and what they have not. Detailed information on how automation drives and measures the system helps avoid this problem.

Better communication enables more efficient collaboration

MetaAutomation records all the information about how automation drives and measures the SUT, in a hierarchical structure.[30] Automation can therefore create much richer knowledge of SUT behavior and performance than before, whether the check passes or fails. The format of this information makes it accessible from the business language down to the simple, indivisible, single-point-of-potential-failure atomic steps of driving and measuring the SUT. The information thus becomes knowledge for the team to augment and streamline communication about the SUT, across teams or geographies.

QA team

False positive rate

Given a correctly configured Smart Retry engine,[31] the false negative rate will approach zero. False negatives will still occur due to timeouts that might benefit from adjustment in the checks[32] but those timeouts may be related to external dependencies of the system or configuration issues so will tend to be directed as action items to the QA role.

Automation technique

This book gives clear instructions for designing checks. This will lead to more congruence across the efforts of different members of the QA team, and less wasted time.

Debugging time

Full and usable information on how automation drives and measures the SUT, whether a check passes or fails, gives much more clarity in the result (i.e., the artifact of the check run) on root cause of any failed check. This can reduce or even eliminate expensive debugging time.

---

[30] The samples use valid XML for this. XML is the most robust solution at this time.

[31] See the diagrams and discussion of the Smart Retry Solution on pages 143-148.

[32] Timeout values can be edited in the XML that is the result of one check run and the data that drives the next one. Run and make changes to any of the samples to see how this works. The figure on page 165 shows this.

Key to project success

This book goes beyond getting better and more actionable quality information from the system — and faster — to *also* communicate it around the team and across geographically distributed groups in a way that distinct roles can access to see exactly what the SUT is doing. The QA role gains more importance and visibility as the key to project success.

Developers

MetaAutomation gives guidance to vastly improve the speed and value of quality measurements, and communications about that quality, as you are building the software. Your agility, speed, and velocity can achieve new heights.

Developers have a very important, demanding, and difficult job, and from the developers' perspective, it is easy to take it on faith for a while that the beautiful system you are building will deliver just what the client needs.[33] Imagine though, after the unit tests pass for a change set, you have a set of fast, scalable bottom-up and system verifications that validate your beautiful product with system dependencies in place. Imagine that these checks can all happen in less than five minutes to validate your change set, not just for your unit, but for the whole team, before your changes can affect anyone else on your team.

The full realization of the product you are building is more complex than just the code you own, and more complex than the code that the whole dev team owns; it fits into the information ecosystem, including the whole internet and the culture of systems, services and/or end-users who are the ultimate customers of your product. It is useful to an extent to be idealistic about quality for your product, but it is helpful to be reminded often, and with good, actionable information, how your system fits into that larger ecosystem of human culture and information.

What does "quality" mean for your product? The question is very open-ended. Many aspects of quality involve interactions with externalities that are simply beyond your control; therefore, frequent, fast, and scalable verifications in a system setting are very important. Even if your unit tests reach 100% code coverage, you still need those system tests to measure and communicate product quality according to what your customers would see or interact with.

As James Coplien wrote,

> *In most businesses, the only tests that have business value are those that are derived from business requirements. (Coplien 2014)*

You are probably aware of system automation efforts that have failed due to long-running tests, tests that fail intermittently, tests that do not deliver useful information any more than "something passed, but we're not confident exactly what" or "something

---

[33] I know, I have performed this role extensively.

failed, but we don't know exactly what, let's see if we can reproduce it." MetaAutomation fixes these issues by focusing on what automated verifications do well, the business reasons for those verifications, how these can run faster and more efficiently and without false positives,[34] and not dropping useful, actionable information as conventional automation does.

If your project has a QA team, you know that despite best intentions from team participants, some antagonism can come from misalignment of objectives: the developers are pushed to deliver functionality fast, and the QA people are motivated to find bugs, which, when found, can appear to slow the developers down. MetaAutomation adds the perspective and enables the functionality to put bugs in their place; finding bugs is no longer the most important work that QA can do. With MetaAutomation, QA helps developers work faster.

MetaAutomation guides the team to create fast, repeatable verifications of the business requirements of the software product, including the behavioral requirements but also including perf, negative behaviors, etc. The pure-data artifacts of the check runs clearly document functional requirements. Even better, these artifacts are available to the whole team in views customized for the viewer and analysis over a build or over the entire time span in the Software Development Lifecycle (SDLC) that a given behavior was measured.

Anyone on the team can look at what the product does in terms of customer deliverables, and even drill down into the data to see what steps took place in a check and how many milliseconds the step took as part of a specific check run.[35] MetaAutomation shows how to make all this self-documenting in pure and structured data. If a given step for a given check needs more data, a data element can be added in check code. Check steps are hierarchical, so the self-documenting of the steps is flexible and deep enough to prevent mission creep in the steps (as happens in, e.g., keyword-driven testing).

Leadership sees in detail what the developers are delivering, as does everybody on the team. Transparency spans the team. Communication is much easier, more accurate, and precise. Trust improves as a result, making everybody's job easier.

False positive rate
With much better data from the SUT, the quality automation system can be smart about sending notifications. False positives as experienced by developers — where a dev gets an email about a failure, but it is

---

[34] "False positives" are check failures that appear actionable to people on the team, at least briefly, but it takes some human effort to determine that they are not actionable. See also false positive in the glossary on page 221.

[35] Try running any of the samples and viewing the results in an XML-supporting browser to see this in action. The samples are on pages 161-176.

really an action item for the QA role — are reduced to near zero.

Work faster

This book shows how to scale check runs and deliver highly trustworthy quality data, so knowledge of quality issues is available faster. Check-in gates can include many system tests to reduce the chance of the developer team being disrupted by breaking changes.

Product code

MetaAutomation makes no demands on product code other than what you would do anyway to create testable code. Good and modular architecture is just as important as it always is, with services, an SDK, or an API to access the business logic. Instrumentation as needed in the code to expose information at runtime (with security considerations, of course) and GUIs with locale-independent identifiers for displayed objects, are all things that help product testability, no matter the tool or method used for automated verifications.

Manual testers

For the same reason that MetaAutomation reduces defect escapes,[36] manual testers can concentrate on what they enjoy and do well: intelligent exploratory testing and other things that cannot be automated. Rather than cycling through repetitive "test cases," anyone doing manual testing can see exactly what the automation did and what automation measured, so they can focus on what still needs to be measured and explored.

Leads and managers

Leaders have complete visibility into how automation drives and measures the SUT. An intranet site lets them drill down from the business-facing steps at the higher levels of the hierarchy, if they choose, all the way down to the atomic steps of driving and measuring the system. Through this kind of exploration, they also have unprecedented clarity into the work that the developers and the QA people are doing, and unprecedented clarity into failures with the automation as they occur or system behavior over time throughout most of the SDLC.

Executive suite and accounting

For a software company, the SUT is an important asset. Leaders can answer questions like "How complete is the product? How good is it? Are we progressing towards product ship as expected?" in much more detail on product behavior and performance.[37]

In the age of Sarbanes-Oxley (SOX), investors will appreciate the added speed, time resolution, fidelity, and completeness in valuing software assets under development.

---

[36] See "Low false negative rate" above on page 23.

[37] The value that MetaAutomation offers is complementary to analytics.

Benefits for different team structures

Agile teams

Agile puts a high value on communication and transparency, in the interest of moving fast and potentially changing direction.

With MetaAutomation, automation driving the SUT *documents itself* in detail so there is no need for people to create or edit documents on detailed product behavior, or test cases. Less work creating and maintaining documentation supports agility. The knowledge created by the automation is easily accessible on, e.g., an intranet site, and independent of geography, and available to any team member concerned with product behavior, functional quality, or performance.

Fast feedback with detail supports agility because the team can move faster. MetaAutomation supports notifications on product quality issues, sent only to people who need to know, rather than a broad discussion list. The result is that actionable notifications are more trustworthy and so the team acts on them faster.

See pages 28-29 for more on requirements.

MetaAutomation does require prioritized business and functional requirements. They must be available to the team. See the Prioritized Requirements pattern on pages 77-83. The Atomic Check pattern needs the checks to link to requirements.[38]

If your team does not discuss, record, and prioritize requirements, you might not know what you are building or why.

Combined engineering

The benefits of MetaAutomation apply equally well when people have roles that cross developer and QA: speed, detailed communication, targeted notifications on actionable check failures, and deep, detailed, and accessible information on how automation drives and measures the product.

Distributed teams

With MetaAutomation, automation that drives the product documents itself and how it drives and measures the product at runtime. It is very detailed, highly trustworthy, and enables drill-down from the business-facing steps near the root of the hierarchy to the atomic steps at the leaves that drive and measure the SUT.[39]

Automation generates the information in the lab or the cloud and is all available on the intranet to give unprecedented clarity into what the SUT is doing and what remote team members are doing. Other forms of communication still need to happen, but the clarity and detail on product behavior make them more efficient.

---

[38] Atomic Check is on pages 99-119.

[39] Try running any of the samples and viewing the results in an XML-supporting browser to see this in action. The samples are on pages 161-176.

Benefits by software project type

Internet of things (IoT)

Sample 3 (pages 173-176) shows checks that run across multiple tiers and give the same detailed information from every tier. With modification, the code and deployment can run across any number of tiers. Business requirements that might otherwise take several separate tests or checks, with faked or stubbed interfaces *and* the extra work and quality risk that would result, can now validate with just one check. The result is faster, better, and more detailed information, with less quality risk.

Web or GUI Client

Automation on web clients might have race conditions due to JavaScript and/or browser AJAX requests. A GUI client has similar problems. There are tricks and tools to synchronization, but automated procedures on the SUT tend to be slow and can be flaky.

There might be a good application for API or bottom-up testing techniques (page 29) to speed checks on deeper business-logic requirements to find the higher-risk issues sooner. Also, the Check patterns, Precondition Pool, and Parallel Run patterns will help make the checks faster and more scalable.

For automation on web clients, MetaAutomation and specifically the Smart Retry pattern solve the flaky check problem.[40]

Benefits for quality practices

Analytics and synthetics

If there is telemetry or product instrumentation to support analytics, the log entries that serve as instrumentation in the product can be redirected and reused during check runs to supplement data generated during the check. The check can record product internals and persist them in the hierarchy of the check result,[41] so make them available for viewing, query, and analysis.

TDD

Test-driven development (TDD) in the general sense, i.e., writing the test before implementing the feature, is compatible with MetaAutomation.[42]

MetaAutomation is about system tests that trace to functional requirements, to help the entire team and the development process.

On the other hand, unit tests (that are often used with TDD) are out of scope for this book. Please see more on unit tests on pages 203-204.

Requirements

The Prioritized Requirements pattern is in this book because if requirements are not well understood, there may be chaos on the team, and certainly the resulting product is unlikely to be very good. If the team does

---

[40] See Smart Retry on pages 141-150.
[41] This would require persistence and synchronization techniques.

[42] Of course, this is limited to the extent that interfaces or design elements are known in advance.

not discuss, agree on, and record requirements, then people on the team do not know what they are building.[43]

This does not conflict with agile practices, if the documentation is well structured, accessible, and not repetitive.

Robin Goldsmith again:

> *A … bit of conventional wisdom is that requirements keep changing and can't possibly be known up-front. Well, when we look at these changes from a different perspective, we realize that* it's really our awareness of the requirements, rather than the requirements themselves, that accounts for much of the apparent change.[44] *(Goldsmith 2004, p. 9)*

Having fast and detailed feedback on functional quality for the SUT requires a good, prioritized set of requirements.

API or bottom-up testing

Douglas Hoffman told me that, compared to testing with a client GUI, service or API checks will run at least ten times faster.[45] He later clarified: this was an understatement. This is consistent with my experience, and it makes sense: the overhead of running a GUI is significant.[46]

Another advantage of testing below the GUI is that, on a failure, the information available through an exception and stack trace is much more detailed than what one could get through a GUI.

See Figure 27 on page 108 for the relationship between quality risk and dependencies.

The benefits of these practices are greatly amplified by the detailed behavioral information from the SUT, as enabled by the techniques of MetaAutomation.

Performance testing

The samples (pages 161-176) show that every step in the hierarchy gets milliseconds to completion. Performance information is always present in the artifacts of a check run, and available for analysis.

The Extension Check pattern on pages 125-128 enables a fast and flexible approach to verifications of performance standards. Load or stress tests can reuse checks implemented by the Atomic Check pattern.[47]

Model-based testing

Long-running tests such as complex model-based tests are useful for finding bugs that are difficult to find any other way. If the team writes these tests using the self-documenting automation code presented with this book,[48] then the artifact of the run will document in detail the steps taken, measurements made and other data. A tool can then analyze or reduce the results to

---

[43] See Prioritized Requirements on pages 77-83.
[44] Emphasis is in the original.
[45] I spoke with Douglas at PNSQC 2011.

[46] See more on GUI testing on page 28.
[47] See Atomic Check on pages 99-119.
[48] See the samples on pages 161-176.

the simplest sequence that would reproduce the issue.

Product instrumentation and analytics

As Paul Gerrard noted

> *Analytics cannot shield end-users from failures. (Gerrard 2016a)*

The information from analytics can lead to great business value. This information cannot be gathered any other way. But, to avoid breaking customers' experiences with the product (as with Figure 5 on page 32) or interrupt the work of developers on the team the team still must validate, quickly, repeatedly, and reliably, that the system still does what the team needs it to do.

Figure 4 below shows that automation can reuse analytics' product instrumentation to augment SUT data during a check run.

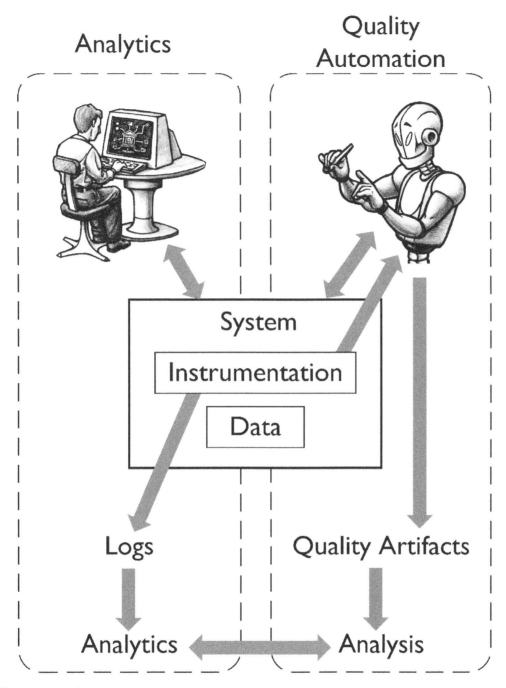

Fig. 4. Showing synergy between analytics and quality automation.

A/B testing

For web sites or other cloud-enabled applications, A/B testing is a powerful technique for measuring the impact of changes on customers or turning features on for them.[49]

Fig. 5. Without quality automation, A/B testing can break customers

---

[49] Assuming that quality has been measured with the feature flag in both "on" and "off" states, before issues can impact customers.

However, it is a terrible way to test whether requirements are met or whether a set of changes break customers' experience, because in those cases, it needs customers to have their experience broken with the app (or lose some customer data, be exposed to security risks etc.) before the team becomes aware. That is much too late. When the customer's experience is broken (shown in Figure 5 opposite) your company suffers loss of goodwill, lost customers, and maybe bad press too.

To answer the question "Does the system do what we need it to do?" definitively, fast, with high recall and precision, you need MetaAutomation.

Manual test

Automation creates artifacts to document itself in approachable, detailed ways and since the result is highly trustworthy there is no need for manual testing on those measurements. The artifacts show exactly what automation measures, so what is *not* measured is clear by omission. The negative spaces of "not measured" SUT aspects give targets for more checks or exploratory manual testing.

Test cases

In the context of automated quality measurements, test cases are obsoleted. The automation code documents itself in detail; other than the code itself, there is nothing to record or maintain.

For quality aspects that cannot be automated, the team can document parts of the SUT and general things to look for, but these would look more like guides to exploratory testing than test case scripts.

Shift left testing

The functional part of Shift Left testing is about verifying correct behavior in the SUT as early as possible (i.e., towards the left on the timeline view).

This could mean using unit tests as soon as a unit is implemented; however, unit tests have limited value.[50]

MetaAutomation addresses Shift Left with very fast and repeatable checks, and bottom-up testing.[51]

Data-driven testing

"Active" data that drives checks is a powerful technique to reuse check code with various input data, or test user accounts, etc. and create many repeatable checks.

The samples (pages 161-176) support reading and writing data in XML child elements in the check artifact. Developers can extend the sample implementation code to support data-driven checks.

DevOps and continuous everything

Humble and Farley's "Continuous Delivery" book of 2011 made a promise:

> *This book describes how to revolutionize software delivery by*

---

[50] Please see the appendix "Unit Tests" on pages 203-204.

[51] See the section "API or bottom-up testing" on page 29.

making the path from idea to realized business value – the cycle time – shorter and safer. (Humble and Farley 2011, p. xxiv)

The authors use a deep understanding of the software creation process and apply automation to describe an idea to ship software faster and cheaper. This is good stuff, and the corresponding movement in the software industry is quite successful.

On the other hand, there is significant opportunity cost implied in their Chapter 8 "Automated Acceptance Testing." Talk of business-facing acceptance tests and repeatable automation is good, and the use of "executable" specifications to improve communication with stakeholders is a promising idea, but unfortunately, it does not go far enough, and it has other issues. Please see the section on BDD[52] for more discussion on this and how MetaAutomation answers the shortcomings of keyword-driven automation.

MetaAutomation complements DevOps and Continuous Integration, Deployment, Delivery etc. by applying automation to get faster, more complete, and more trustworthy feedback on the system, and using automation to integrate quality and communications around the larger team. It helps DevOps and continuous everything work better by giving better and more

trustworthy quality feedback faster and more effectively around the team.

Humble and Farley again:

It is essential that everybody involved in the process of delivering software is involved in the feedback process. (Humble and Farley 2011, p.15)

MetaAutomation helps reach that dream through unprecedented ease and detail of communication about what automation drives the SUT to do.

Obviated quality practices

Behavioral driven development (BDD)

Humble and Farley wrote

Tools like Cucumber, JBehave, Concordion, Twist, and FitNesse allow you to put acceptance criteria directly in tests and link them to the underlying implementation. (Humble and Farley 2011, p.191)

The automated tests are in what they described as "executable Specifications" if the script, using something like the "given, when, then" format.[53] "Given" is the precondition, "when" is the procedure, and "then" is the verification. It is a neat idea and, in theory, an improvement in clarity for the team on what the automation is doing with the SUT.

Unfortunately, it needs a custom script language *and* an interpreter for that language. "Glue code" must implement the

---

[52] See section "Behavioral driven development (BDD)" on pages 34-35.

[53] This could be the language called Gherkin.

keywords and verbs, causing opacity at the implementation level; the glue code does not document itself. The keywords document themselves when they execute, but what happens between the keyword and the SUT? Unless one is willing to inspect source code (and use a debugger to step through if it is at all complicated) that is a mystery. It might even be doing nothing, and the customer of that information does not know. It might also be doing something unexpected or inconsistent. I know from personal experience (with the open-source tool Robot Framework) that sometimes, modifications to a keyword implementation are needed just to make the keyword reusable.[54]

With BDD, the keywords are at one level of abstraction: probably the business logic level. If one wants more detail on what is going on with automation driving the SUT, one must go inspect and/or debug automation source code.

As Computer Science professor Robert Biddle wrote

> ...I was always interested in FITnesse, and the efforts it made to open tests to product-owners. I think it was unsuccessful but valiant... (Biddle 2017)

MetaAutomation gives tools and techniques so that drill-down into details of actual automation-SUT interactions is available to anyone on the team who cares about quality. It needs no custom script language, nor an interpreter. Code driving the SUT documents itself directly in a robust format, from atomic steps. The working samples (pages 161-176) show how this works.

Supplementary reading

Goldsmith on requirements

Robin Goldsmith wrote an excellent book on discovering, recording, and changing requirements: "Discovering REAL Business Requirements for Software Project Success." That book is also in the references section at the end of this one.

Review Questions

The answers are on pages 205-206.

1) Describe two values to the business that quality automation delivers, but the manual test role cannot.
2) Why is the manual test role still important?
3) What is wrong with the phrase "test automation?"
4) What is a basic value that MetaAutomation can bring to the entire team, even a geographically distributed one?
5) Name some important values that MetaAutomation can bring to DevOps practices.
6) How does MetaAutomation make manual testing more productive?

---

[54] This is called "keyword drift."

Chapter 4
The Three Paradigm Shifts

The leap in quality productivity that MetaAutomation describes is only accessible by looking at the quality automation space in a new way.

Paradigms are important for organizing ideas. As Kuhn writes,

> *In the absence of a paradigm or some candidate for paradigm, all of the facts that could possibly pertain to the development of a given science are likely to seem equally relevant. (Kuhn 1962, p.15)*

Kuhn goes on to describe the "morass" of ideas that could result in the absence of a paradigm. By contrast,

> *Acquisition of a paradigm ... is a sign of maturity in the development of any given scientific field. (Kuhn 1962, p.12)*

This book is more technology than science, but the paradigms of software quality that give foundations for communication and understanding are equally valid as such.

The changes presented in this book distill down to three shifts from old, established paradigms to new ones that are more empowering to the software development team and the business.

The first one is the most radical and basic, and the most challenging, [55] but it brings immediate returns as well as much larger opportunities to the business. The second and third paradigm shifts build on the first.

---

[55] Note however that the samples described on pages 161-176 make the challenge much easier. They are open-source and implement a robust solution to the most complex part of the basis for MetaAutomation.

Given the new perspectives on the practice of functional software quality with automation – plus, performance and reliability quality as well –

MetaAutomation, the pattern language, presents prescriptive patterns as structures that guide an implementation.

Chapter 5

Paradigm Shift One: Bring Value from All Functional Quality Data

This shift is from the automation losing data on the SUT – that is, dropping most of the business-actionable information on the floor – to recording all this data in a robust structure that supports rich automation.

Old Paradigm: Use Log Statements to Get a Smattering of Product Data

With conventional automation, if one wants information back from the product, one uses log statements.[56] This is better than nothing, but still misses most of the information and therefore most of the value.

Test is NOT just about finding bugs

With the conventional approach, in case of check "pass," all that the QA people are looking for is a green bubble or some other Boolean sign. Other than the fact that the SUT behaves correctly according to whatever automation drives the SUT to do, people do not care much.

Conventional automation drops most product data on the floor (see Figure 7 on page 42) but there is something else going on: many people deny this in my experience, but the way they talk about the business value of automation betrays the fact that they are influenced by the historical accident in Myers' 1979 book.[57]

The attitude "We only care about bugs" devalues the results of automation if it passes, because if the automation passes, it has not (apparently) found any bugs, by Myers' book there is no value, and so the

---

[56] In case of failure, there is a stack trace and maybe some other limited information about the system at exception throw.

[57] See the discussion "The Tyranny of Bugs" on pages 16-18.

team does not care. Figure 6 shows this below.

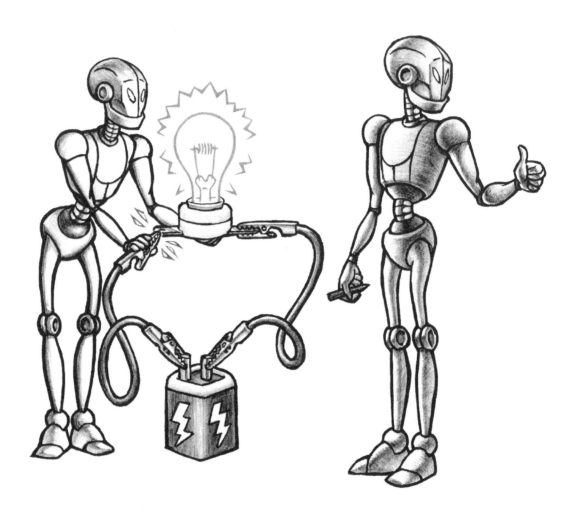

Fig. 6. Conventional "test automation" drops actionable information and only gives Boolean results for a pass.

See the testing type diagram again on page 17: bugs are important, but to help the team move forward with the product, and to ensure that it does, the team needs repeatable automation and it needs to know how the automation drives and measures the SUT.

For examples of software that matters to people, we can look to software quality practices at places like NASA and Japan's JAXA. In a 2014 paper, Dan Port et al. wrote

> *We depart from contemporary views that focus on defect-centric factors such as defect avoidance or early defect mitigation. Rather, we have observed that assurance value stems from enabling more confident quality-critical decision making… from this viewpoint, assurance value does not depend on the actual number of defects found; instead it depends on the degree of coverage an assurance activity provides, regardless if defects are found.* (Port 2014)

Opportunity costs are not always obvious. In conventional approaches to "test automation," the opportunity cost of dropping data on how the SUT is being driven, how it responds and how long the system takes to respond, includes all the values offered by MetaAutomation. This cost happens because of the ways in which "test automation" is not capable of persisting more than a small bit of this data.

Suppose a team member is filling the usual QA role of writing automation to drive the SUT and wishes to record feedback from the SUT as automation drives it. Log statements are better than nothing, but logs focus on recording distinct and isolated events. By design, other than through timestamps, relationships between log statements do not exist. People can cobble together other relationships, however, with session IDs or other logged system state, but still, almost all of the data is dropped.[58]

People doing manual test see all this, though: how they drive the SUT, and the response, and the performance (although with much less precision). This book is, in part, about the awesome power of having automation do something similar — with much more detail and accuracy. Conventional practices are only barely capable of recording all this data, and it is not for lack of trying; BDD attempts to do this but falls short due to a persistent layer of obscurity underneath the keywords and verbs that it uses to drive and measure the SUT.

---

[58] See Figure 7 below.

Fig. 7. "Test automation" drops most of the business value on the floor.

Some of the data dropped on the floor with "test automation" can be recovered later with laborious and expensive manual testing or a manual debugging through a failure. The team might dig the information up *much* *later* through product instrumentation after it breaks the experience of an end-user with the software product.[59] But, time is important here. To ship software faster and at higher quality, the team must be able to collect good, detailed, and precise quality data fast and repeatedly. That's what this book is about.

Logs are the ideal tool for a different problem domain

Logs are simple to implement, lightweight, and very fast. They are perfect for recording events on web servers, power company equipment, and other processes that are meant to run continuously for a very long time.

Automated checks are limited in time. They have procedures with steps, a well-defined beginning, and an end.

How the steps form a complete check is important, and the relationship of those steps to each other is important, too. For a check of any complexity, the hierarchical relationship between the steps is important context.

By design, logs are very poor at establishing relationship between events. They are an ideal tool for web servers handing events, but very poor for getting information about the execution of a procedure.

The problem of scope

One way to try to create context between listed statements is to make all or most of the log statements at a similar scope compared to the business logic of the automation driving the SUT. But this creates another problem: what about a higher-level scope, closer to the business? That can be cobbled together, but it is not always clear because more technology-facing detail might be hidden.

Creating an interpreted language to drive the SUT, e.g., BDD/Gherkin, has the same problem: The keywords, verbs, etc. that are the elements of the language must go at a scope between the business and the technology. Other scopes may lose information.

To record all the information, at all scopes *including* the business-facing language at the highest level of generality, the technology-facing steps that drive the SUT, and every level in between, you need the structure that Hierarchical Steps provides.[60]

New Paradigm: Record Complete and Context-Rich Steps and Measurements

One of the points that Collins and Lucena Jr. make towards managing quality risk in an agile environment is to

> *Use test automation for documentation and information feedback. (Collins and Lucena Jr 2012, p.62)*

MetaAutomation shows how to do that with unprecedented depth, detail, and trustworthiness. Its structure supports automation for powerful benefit to the business.

---

[59] See Figure 5 on page 32.

[60] For more information, see the Hierarchical Steps pattern on pages 85-98.

Recording all that is going on with the SUT

The importance of data to business – all kinds of businesses – is a persistent meme these days. Most of the data of driving and measuring the SUT was unavailable to automation in a usable form, until now.

We have an opportunity to persist and realize the value of all functional quality data, including performance and reliability, both in case of pass and fail. This is the basis for MetaAutomation and all the business value to be realized as a result.

For a multi-step procedure, steps have context; the relationship of a step to some other steps is very important.

For example, suppose a check fails. With effective recording of how automation drives and measures the SUT, root cause is clear from the perspective of the code driving the product. If the check fail becomes an action item for a developer, it is highly actionable because all the data is already there; in fact, the developer might not need to even reproduce the problem.

As Davies and Roper noted in their 2014 paper

> *The way in which a bug is reported is clearly of importance to the developer charged with fixing the bug, as it can have a big impact on the ease with which they may be able to fix the bug. However, this information is also of wider interest and impacts on a number of important activities from mining bug repositories for*

> *information, through developing tools to support activities such as bug localisation, to building the next generation of bug tracking systems. Knowledge of what information that is reported, the way in which it is reported and how frequently it appears will have a significant influence on all these activities. (Davies and Roper 2014)*

The same paper notes on that the #1 most important bit of information that developers want is "steps to reproduce."

This book shows how to get those in unprecedented and highly trustworthy detail, in a business-friendly or ubiquitous language of the domain experts, from code that documents itself as it runs. See the Solution to the Hierarchical Steps pattern (pages 88-91) for more on how ubiquitous language is used for a self-documenting check procedure.

Repeatable procedures are bounded in time

Web servers respond to events, and by design, the faster and more simply they do respond, the better. Logs are therefore ideal for reporting from a web server.

By contrast, the repeatable multi-step procedure of a check is bound by a beginning and an end. This presents an opportunity: the artifacts, that is, results from a check run, can now have a structure that naturally preserves contextual information for later use. This calls for a hierarchical format that is more pure data, less presentation.

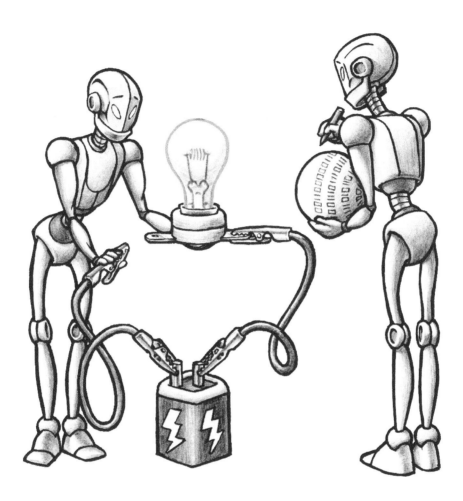

Fig. 8. MetaAutomation captures system interactions in a useful, actionable format.

The samples described by this book use XML. Every check creates, at completion, an XML document to represent the check steps and other collected data on the SUT. As compared to a linear list of log statements, such XML is much more efficient and robust for analysis after the run of the check is complete.[61]

Hierarchical steps are natural

The Hierarchical Steps pattern is a foundation for MetaAutomation.[62] The pattern exists in human culture. In fact, we all do it, every time we do something that is not completely trivial, and every time we record or communicate it.

For example, this morning I went to the grocery store. I do not think about this with a long, linear list of steps (for example, "Step 1: put on shoes," "Step 2: grab key fob," etc.), I think about the *high* level first, which could be stated as "get bananas." Then I think about how; walk, ride a bike, or drive my electric car? This gives the next level of detail with five steps: Prepare to leave house, drive there, buy bananas, drive back, resume my work. Eventually, every one of these five steps need more detail, for example, when I buy bananas there is more detail: enter grocery store, find bananas, put bananas in basket, proceed to cashier, pay, leave store. Every one of these steps has more detail, for example, the "pay" step: pay with debit card, get cash back, get bananas (perhaps in a sack). Every one of those steps might have more details, even if nobody has bothered to write them down.

If I were to record this procedure as if I were doing it for a computer, assuming complete ignorance (remember, computers are dumb), doing it with a long linear list of steps would be awkward and difficult, and I would miss many details. Fortunately, with the Hierarchical Steps pattern, adding more detail is easy; we figure it out on the fly or we ask someone for advice, and if recording the procedure, we do that by adding child nodes to the hierarchy without changing anything else.

Implementing the hierarchy is complex, so I did this for you with code that you can copy, change, or port to other languages or platforms.[63] The steps of a check are now self-documenting in a hierarchy, so there is much better data from a check artifact and much more closely linked to the implementation – therefore, more trustworthy – than even keyword-driven automation or Gherkin/BDD tools. As a bonus, each step in the hierarchy remembers its own milliseconds-to-completion, so performance testing is built-in.

This is very useful; in fact, as performance quality guru Mark Tomlinson told me

> *For roughly 80% of client needs, the millisecond-to-completion of an operation is sufficient for people interested in performance, and none of the CPU or memory load or network bandwidth is needed. (Tomlinson 2017a)*

---

[61] XML is not part of the Hierarchical Steps pattern, nor the Atomic Check pattern, but it is excellent choice as a metalanguage to manage the hierarchy.

[62] See the Hierarchical Steps pattern on pages 85-98.

[63] See the working software samples, pages 161-176.

The top-level steps – for example, the "get bananas" from above – conveniently face the business. This is how people generally think about and communicate the problem. Drilling down through the child steps of the hierarchy gives more detail, all the way down to the "leaf" steps which have no children of their own — at least, for procedures that people carry out, no details which people have bothered to record.[64]

For quality automation, the leaves of the hierarchy are atomic steps. These are the technology-facing steps. This duality between business-facing and technology-facing is a useful organization to make actual data on what the SUT is driven to do available to everybody, including the parameters and measurements, and SUT instrumentation as needed. The clarity on SUT behavior unifies the larger team, even across roles or across geographies.

As Parveen et al. note

> *The key to effective test management is communication among different parties involved in the process. (Parveen et al. 2007, p.86)*

Hierarchical Steps, and code that documents itself at runtime, enables richer and more trustworthy communication than previously possible.

More detail on this is in the Hierarchical Steps pattern (pages 88-91), Atomic Check pattern (pages 99-119), and in the software samples (pages 161-176).

Replace code comments with something better

As automation architect Paul Grizzaffi put it,

> *code comments are as important as the code itself. (Grizzaffi 2018)*

Comments, at one level of abstraction (i.e., generality) higher than the code itself, are important for code readability and maintainability. But, what if something much better could replace them in non-shipping automation code?

A compiler strips code comments out (an interpreter just ignores them) so they have no effect at runtime. With MetaAutomation, check steps have descriptive names as hard-coded strings. The runtime records the names in the hierarchy of steps that is the backbone for the check result. The names are an improvement over code comments because they describe the step in code *and* they document themselves at runtime in a rich context.

Fix the false positive problem

If a check result is a "Fail," but on investigation the "Fail" is *not* actionable by the team, the event can be disruptive. As Herzig and Nagappan wrote in their 2015 paper on handling false test alarms

---

[64] Try running any of the samples and viewing the results in an XML-supporting browser to see this in action.

False test alarms are expensive and harm the verification and development process without providing any benefit. (Herzig and Nagappan 2015)

With all the SUT behavior data available, there is no longer any need for someone in the QA role to try to reproduce a failure and debug through to find enough details to choose whether to report a bug. The time and the cost for this are no longer needed. The quality automation system has enough information to notify those who need to know quickly when it finds quality issues (as with the Automated Triage pattern on pages 151-154).

Quality automation handles non-actionable false positives by preventing them from interrupting team members' work.[65] For example, suppose there is a timeout on an external dependency.[66] A smart retry of the check might pass. Automation preserves all the data on the timeout, but it is not an immediate action item, and it need not interrupt anyone's workflow.

Fix the defect escape/false negative problem

When all the details of driving and measuring the SUT are persisted, in data that is robust, complete and queryable, on study and deep knowledge of the SUT, it becomes clear what is *not* measured. The chances of a false negative, also called a defect escape, is reduced; all software products that are well-tested ship with bugs, and often customers find issues, but the chance of a surprise where the team responds "But, we thought we tested that!" does not happen. What is measured (and not) with automation is very clear, detailed, and available to everybody on the team.

The end of Beizer's Pesticide Paradox

Beizer's Pesticide Paradox states

Every method you use to prevent or find bugs leaves a residue of subtler bugs against which those methods are ineffectual. (Beizer 1990, p.9)

With conventional "test automation" this is a real problem. With MetaAutomation and the vastly better clarity on how automation drives and measures the SUT, at least it is knowable — based on inspection of the product and the check artifacts — exactly what gaps are left by the automated checks. The "residue of subtler bugs" becomes discoverable.

The First Paradigm Shift Enables the Second

This first paradigm shift – recording all the data of driving and measuring the SUT, in an accessible and automation-friendly structure – enables the second paradigm shift: bringing value to the whole team. The QA role, or whoever wrote the automation, never has to interpret the automation manually to the business, even in the case of a failure. When the data is highly detailed, context-rich, and

---

[65] See Smart Retry on pages 141-150.

[66] For example, this could be a request of an external web service.

trustworthy, people on the team — managers, designers, and those who would not normally be interested in automation — can access the data from the SUT in a way that is meaningful to them.

Anyone can go to the team quality portal[67] and drill down on a check result, from the business-facing steps at the top to the technology-facing steps at the bottom.

Also, the rich and structured data from implementing Hierarchical Steps supports rich quality automation to help the whole team be more productive and responsive on product quality.

While "test automation" only helps the QA role be more productive (but with significant risk – see Chapter 3 "Fixing "Test Automation"" on pages 11-22), automation that saves data in a useful structure benefits the whole team.

The First Paradigm Shift Enables the Third

With all data from driving and measuring the SUT, as part of a complete and configured system, the Smart Retry pattern (pages 141-150) eliminates false positives. A common justification for stubbing out dependencies goes away. This applies to both external dependencies and inter-tier dependencies for the internet of things.

This means that automation can measure the SUT based on functional requirements,

without the quality risk that comes from skipping over dependencies. One reason this is important: outside the developer role, unit tests are not meaningful. Unless the unit is an algorithm that is surfaced in product behavior and is important to the business, they do not relate to requirements.[68]

The larger software team will want quality data of the SUT as it relates to the ecosystem (if the ecosystem exists), and with MetaAutomation they can get it, in robust detail including performance.

Sample 3 (pages 173-176) shows how a check can cross tiers, for the internet of things. Given that all the product driving and measurement data is preserved, the structure that makes this possible also makes it possible to do it across tiers. The whole SUT and ecosystem are represented together to support Paradigm Shift Three.

---

[67] Quality portal is defined in the glossary on page 223. This is what I generically call an implementation of the Queryable Quality pattern on pages 155-158.

[68] E.g., with business-oriented algorithms such as encryption or compression.

Review Questions

The answers are on pages 206-207.

1) What historical accident encourages complacency that a green bubble is all the team needs to know about a passed check?

2) What property of logs and log statements make them ideal for product instrumentation, but a poor fit for collecting data on a procedure in non-shipping code?

3) Name some simple advantages of recording all the data of driving and measuring the SUT, in a highly trustworthy way, and in a structure that saves context and enables rich and robust analysis.

Chapter 6
Paradigm Shift Two: Bring Value to the Whole Team

The conventional practice of "test automation" helps the QA role be more productive, but with risks.[69]

With this book, I define the term and practice "quality automation" which helps the *whole team* be more productive, not just the QA role, and without those risks.

Old paradigm: "Test Automation" Applies Automation to Help QA Team

The basic idea of "test automation" is automating what a person would otherwise do manually in the QA role.[70] The value of automation appears therefore to be limited to the QA team. The rationale for "test automation" is the idea that the QA team can thereby do its job faster and more cheaply.

Information that the QA team feeds to the rest of the team is limited to whatever structures and reporting that QA does internally. Information on SUT behavior is limited even with the keywords that BDD/Gherkin uses;[71] there is still a lot of detail on product behavior that lives only in QA-owned source code, and the larger team knows it. This reduces confidence in what QA is telling them about the product.

---

[69] See the section "Fixing "Test Automation"" on pages 11-22.

[70] See the section "Linguistic relativity" on pages 14-16.

[71] For more information, see the Old Paradigm of Paradigm Shift one on pages 39-43, and the section on BDD on pages 34-35.

Remember the "test is all about finding bugs?" statement from 1979?[72] This attitude is still pervasive around teams, and it tends to reinforce the limited value that the QA role brings to the rest of the team; after all, if test really were just about finding bugs, then "test automation" would be the same but faster and that is just QA's job, not the concern of the larger team.

Fig. 9. "Test automation" drops most of the information, so QA role must do more manual reporting to leadership.

---

[72] See the section "The Tyranny of Bugs" on pages 16-18.

Even worse, if QA were just about finding bugs, then that limits QA's contribution to one in which they are at odds with the dev role, in the sense that QA may be the bringer of bad news that prevents dev from achieving their delivery targets. Even if team members know, intellectually or through good management, that quality is important, if at some level the QA team is no more than the bringer of bad news, then their reputation and their ability to deliver value to the larger team may be limited. Software quality would suffer.

New Paradigm: Quality Automation Delivers Value Across Larger Team

If I had the power to do it, I would deprecate the term "test automation" because it reduces quality workers' ability to deliver value to their team. Think about "quality automation" instead, and the quality automation problem space; it avoids the overloaded word "test" and specifically addresses what automation can do for quality for the whole team. Quality automation is a topic of this book.

Fig. 10. MetaAutomation gives functional quality information in a robust, approachable, and queryable format, to everybody on the team who cares about SUT quality.

When quality information is traceable to functional requirements (which are traceable to business requirements), and the information is detailed, trustworthy, and accessible to everybody on the team who is concerned with product quality, then everybody has access to exactly what is going on with the SUT. The QA role gets the credit it deserves with high visibility: QA is the team that enables significantly better collaboration and communication around different team roles and even geographically distributed offices. The QA role moves from a peripheral role —

keeping the team honest about quality (or, trying to) — to the central role of measuring and communicating about what the system does, to enable more efficient communication and collaboration around the larger team.

The manual testing role

There may be dedicated manual testers on the team, but all team members do (or, should be doing, at least occasionally) manual test part of the time. The need for this kind of testing never goes away because people are smart, observant, and good detectives. In this area, human intelligence and efficacy will not be matched for a very long time. The team needs manual, human-driven testing.

To add to quality understanding of the SUT, people need to know: has this aspect of SUT behavior already been measured, for this build of the product? If people have limited confidence or clarity into what automation has measured and reported, then there is additional manual testing work needed to cover those aspects of the SUT that automation *might* have covered. This can get repetitive, too, which leads to cost and boredom, and more mistakes and oversights. Think of the drudgery and cost of repeating manual test cases for every build.

People doing manual testing are better at exploratory testing, where there is no script to follow and the answer to the question "Does the SUT do what we need it to do?"

is completely open-ended. That is just more fun, anyway.

Imagine if people doing manual testing had very few "test case" scripts to create, maintain, and follow — or none at all. MetaAutomation enables that because every check that can be automated, *is* automated — close to implementation time — and the checks are completely self-documenting with what automation does with the SUT.[73] Implementing the Queryable Quality pattern[74] makes all that information available to everybody on the team, in a presentation where anyone can open a web page, query on it, find a check, and drill down from the root and the business-facing steps for the check, all the way down to the details. People can see how the SUT was driven and measured, and since it is so detailed and trustworthy, they do not have to repeat any of those verifications. The unknown quality aspects – the ones NOT measured by automation – are the ones for manual testing to explore.

The value to the manual test role, and anyone on the team doing manual testing, is that their job is more efficient and more fun. There is less drudgery. If a tester finds any ambiguity in what is measured, the tester can file a bug on the QA role or fix

---

[73] See the Hierarchical Steps pattern on pages 85-98 and the Atomic Check pattern on pages 99-119.

[74] See the Queryable Quality pattern on pages 155-158.

up the code herself to add that detail to what the check reports.[75]

Clarity and access to the whole team

When people creating the automated checks have linked a check to functional requirement or requirements, implemented the atomic steps, and named them correctly (as the samples demonstrate) they are done communicating to the larger team for those measurements. They do not need to write reports, or maintain test cases, or communicate product quality in any other way. The checks simply document themselves as they run.

The larger team has unprecedented clarity into what the SUT is capable of, what it is driven to do, and how it is measured. For fast repeatable requirements-driven checks that keep quality moving forward, all team members can browse and query for functional quality and performance.

The clarity and visibility work for distributed teams, too, through the quality portal intranet site.[76] Remotely attended meetings become more efficient when they are backed up with trustworthiness and clarity into how the SUT currently behaves.

Blind men and the elephant

The widely retold story of the blind men and the elephant comes from India.

Variations of the story interpret the different perspectives of the men touching and defining various parts of the elephant, and how those perspectives get resolved between the men.

The parable has given insight into the inexpressible nature of truth, the behavior of experts in fields where there is a deficit or inaccessibility of information, the need for communication, and the respect for different perspectives.

Think of the blind men of the parable representing distinct roles in software development. Of course, people developing software are not really blind to the larger picture of the software product. They are smart, well-intentioned, hard-working, and very much aware of the value of good communication. Yet, from the perspective of functional quality and simple performance, with traditional approaches, there remains a deficit in communication and accessibility of information.

This is where the parable applies: by addressing persistence, transparency, automated communications, and accessibility of quality information about the software product, i.e., transparency for this information, MetaAutomation can improve the communication,

---

[75] Ambiguity to what a check step name means can be fixed by renaming it, although this should be avoided because it can affect analysis over time of the artifacts that include that step. Context for a step, including the parent step and any child steps, is always immediately accessible in the artifact of the check run.

[76] See the Queryable Quality pattern on pages 155-158, and the sample portals in sections "Check run in progress" on pages 182-183, and "Check run completed" on pages 183-187.

collaboration, access, and mutual respect around the team.

MetaAutomation brings much greater transparency, vastly better communication, and much more effective management around software quality risk, throughout the larger software development teams. With MetaAutomation in place, quality around functional requirements and performance is equally visible to the QA role, to developers, manual testers, leads and managers, and even the executives if they choose to create or get a quality view customized for them. This improved communication leads to greater collaboration and respect because it brings team members closer together. With transparency, the silo walls come down. Disagreements between the blind men of the parable do not happen anymore.

Team members are happier, too. They have more confidence they are doing good work. Everybody can see on the intranet that functional quality of the SUT reliably and monotonically improves through the SDLC.

The Second Paradigm Shift Leads to the Third

This second paradigm shift is about bringing clarity into product quality and performance around the whole team. Checks link to, and are prioritized by, functional requirements (which link in turn to business requirements). When leaders on the team have access to all that information, they will want to know: are those the real requirements? Are we measuring bits of the SUT in isolation, or are we measuring how it would work for real, as much as currently possible?

The answer drives the third paradigm shift: the fast, repeatable checks that keep quality moving forward do relate to the real, context-aware functional requirements for the product. When relevant, checks interact with dependencies, both inter-tier and external. MetaAutomation makes this possible.

Review Questions

The answers are on page 207.

1) With MetaAutomation, how will cross-role and cross-geography collaboration be faster and more efficient?
2) How does MetaAutomation make the manual testing role be more efficient and enjoyable?
3) What does the approach of this book do to move QA to the center of the software development effort?

Chapter 7

Paradigm Shift Three: Bring Value from the Whole Ecosystem

Old Paradigm: Dependencies Can Be Abstracted Away

A frequent saying among agile developers is "don't test somebody else's code."

With a conventional "test automation" infrastructure, there is time risk to the team that dependencies could show some failure or variance in behavior which would break the automation. Network connections could fail, or third-party services could be variable or could change. If the developer workflow cannot tolerate such things, that could slow them down, so they make stubs or fakes. This is shown metaphorically on the figure on page 60.

From the SDLC perspective, though, doing this creates much bigger and more expensive risks: decoupling dependencies before doing quality measurements means that quality risk of the SUT relationships with those dependencies has been deferred to some point in the future. Risks deferred to the future become more expensive to the business, and potentially *much* more expensive. I have seen it cause a big project to fail. See figure 27 on page 108 for an illustration of quality risk at different levels of dependency.

Testing with dependencies in place is not about testing somebody else's code, it is about testing your own system; does it handle failures related to these systems gracefully? What is the impact to the customer or end-user?

Fig. 11. Quality measurements with faked or stubbed dependencies only measures an incomplete system, so it defers and therefore amplifies quality risk.

Quality is often measured with existing dependencies decoupled for two reasons: performance and reliability. This practice creates quality risks:

- The dependency behavior might change over time

- It might be poorly documented
- The team might misunderstand the dependency behavior
- The team might make errors in faking the dependency

- The dependency might have error conditions that the SUT must handle

If any of those risks pop up late in the SDLC (or worse: discovered by your end-users) then the team has an expensive problem to work through which creates cascading risks.

The practice of faking dependencies *does* have value when errors or other conditions must be injected into dependency behavior for negative testing.

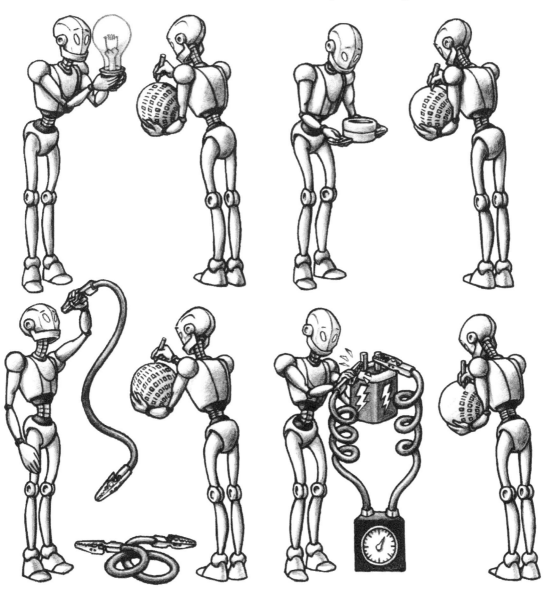

Fig. 12. Unit testing gives information on the units, usually with little or no relationship to functional requirements.

Unit tests aside,[77] MetaAutomation solves both the performance[78] and reliability[79] problems and enables the team to manage

risk proactively and get better quality information on the SUT as it is built.

Fig. 13. Testing without dependencies misses the main product value.

---

[77] See the appendix on Unit Tests on pages 203-204.

[78] Performance issues are solved with the Atomic Check, Event-Driven Check, Extension Check, Precondition Pool, and Parallel Run patterns.

[79] Reliability issues are solved with the Hierarchical Steps, Atomic Check, Event-Driven Check, Extension Check, Smart Retry, and Automated Triage patterns

New Paradigm: Dependencies are Essential to the Quality Ecosystem

A modern connected software system has no value without relationships to dependencies, e.g., different tiers for the Internet of Things or internet services. It follows that there is little value to the team of trying to answer the question "Does the system do what we need it to do?" without those dependencies.

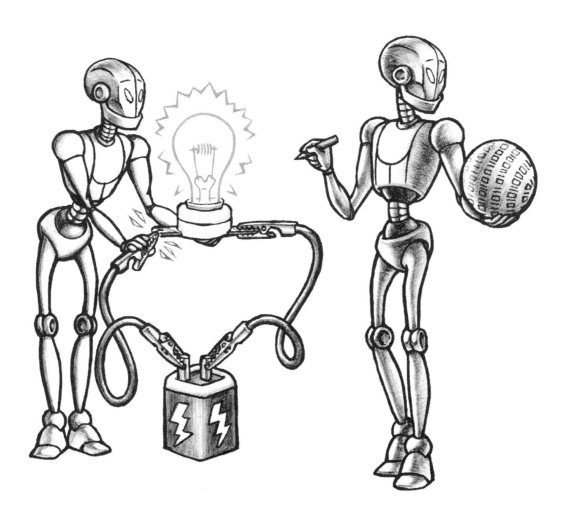

Fig. 14. MetaAutomation records and delivers all information of interaction with the system, for check pass and fail.

Bottom-up or headless testing

Figure 27 on page 108 also shows the value of bottom-up testing for the system.

Bottom-up testing is the practice of testing the less-dependent levels of the product, with all dependencies in place, before or at a higher priority than testing the complete SUT.

Many software systems include a human interface like a web site or a GUI. Distributed products, web sites and services also include defined interfaces such that product components can talk to each other over a network or the internet. Well-architected products often include APIs exported from one executable to another running in the same process, and many products export web services. There are many advantages to automated testing at the lower and less-dependent levels, in addition to complete system testing.

Service or API checks will run much faster than checks that go through a human interface, at least ten times faster.[80]

Automated testing through an API or service returns much better and more actionable information from the product, in case of check failure, than does GUI automation.

Although API or service automation is more abstract because there is no graphical interface to clarify meaning of operations on the product, it can be easier. Programming is much more transparent and simpler, and the compiler is the programmer's friend for quick verifying of types, tokens, structures, etc.

If the automation does not involve a GUI or web browser (or even another user agent) there is much less overhead on the automation client when running the checks. This means that a given amount of computing resources can support more clients, and this gives another way of running more checks.

If the product architecture supports this, the benefits of testing the business logic directly extend even more to the lower levels of the system.

Bottom-up testing reduces product risk by finding or eliminating the most impactful and difficult-to-fix bugs early in the product cycle and doing regression on those issues more quickly and effectively. Lower-level checks give much more detailed and specific information on business-logic behavior.[81]

Testing through the product GUI can find important business-logic bugs, but a graphical interface can also hide business-logic issues by not exposing them, by cluttering issues with bugs specific to the GUI, or even by obscuring them with a bit of corrective code in the GUI layer.

---

[80] This is from a conversation with Douglas Hoffman, although later he said that "ten times faster" was an understatement (Hoffman 2011). This statement is consistent with the author's extensive experience with both types of automation.

[81] See Figure 27 on page 108.

Thorough testing and regression at the lower levels of the product reduces the number of issues that appear in a GUI or web page. As an added benefit, this practice also increases the chance that any issue discovered at the graphical level has root cause at that layer, and not below, which in turn makes it easier and lower-risk to fix.

Any issue with root cause in the GUI layer is low-risk to fix because the lower levels of the application have no dependency on the GUI (assuming good product architecture). As a result, deferring system quality automation that measures a GUI in favor of emphasis on bottom-up testing is a more effective way to manage product risk than doing just system testing of the SUT.

The Atomic Check pattern on pages 99-119 is very well suited to bottom-up, API, and service testing.

Multiple tiers for the Internet of Things

If the SUT has more than one deployment tier, and a functional requirement includes interaction between tiers, include all tiers in the check for that requirement. Sample 3 (pages 173-176) shows how this works, with a check driving and measuring multiple tiers. Driving and measuring the SUT documents itself on all tiers and creates a single XML document at check completion.

External services

To avoid quality risk, the SUT must be tested often and quickly with external dependencies such as services.

The picture of functional quality that the team forms with every run of a set of checks must be consistent, to avoid flaws slipping past one check run only to be uncovered with a later one. The slipped-flaws problem increases quality risk because it means that flaws are not uncovered when they are expected to be measured, but they are discovered later, when the issue becomes harder to fix and there might even be cascading risks. If the check set is run as part of a check-in gate, and the check set run is not consistent, a change set from one developer risks breaking the checks when run by another developer on the team.

If the SUT changes functional behavior based on external data or behavior of an external service, this could interfere with the consistency of the check. Strategies to mitigate this inconsistency and assure fast, consistent quality measurement could include:

- Use a data set that is controlled or constant for the quality automation
- Interact with the service in a way that, for a given check, product behavior is the same
- Measure lower layers of the SUT, for example in the business logic, which do not change in behavior

- See the Event-Driven Check pattern (pages 121-124) for handling external events

When the external service charges a fee for service requests, it can have the effect of delaying quality efforts and therefore creating risk. In that case, the team needs to negotiate a parallel fake service for quality purposes that is free or nearly free. Any business that exports a fee-based service is interested in quality for customers of their service, and therefore it is in their business interest to export a service specifically for quality efforts.

Review Questions

The answers are on pages 207-208.

1) How does the internet make obsolete the practice of testing system in isolation from dependencies?
2) What are some advantages of writing and running checks from the less-dependent layers of the SUT, earlier in the SUT?
3) Name two common reasons for faking or stubbing external dependencies that MetaAutomation obviates.

Section II

The Pattern Language

Chapter 8
Pattern Language: MetaAutomation

From Wikipedia:

> *A pattern language [is] an attempt to express the deeper wisdom of what brings aliveness within a particular field of human endeavor, through a set of interconnected patterns. (Wikipedia, "Pattern Language")*

I created the pattern language MetaAutomation as a guide to achieving an ideal solution to implementing the quality automation space. The beginning patterns described in this book are focused on speed, reliability, and communications.

Richard Gabriel is an established leader in the patterns community, and as he wrote,

> *Patterns… are a means to capture common sense and are a way to capture abstractions that are not easily captured otherwise. (Gabriel 1996, p33)*

MetaAutomation is intended to be a living pattern language, actively used and growing. It could be extended in the future, by me or someone else. Please see the "Future Patterns for MetaAutomation" section on pages 159-160. At this time, it is the only full solution to the quality automation space that I know of, but there may be others in future.

The root of MetaAutomation – the Hierarchical Steps pattern – as applied to the quality automation space in the Atomic Check pattern, is the basis for most of the very powerful aspects of what can be achieved. It is also a quantum leap, because the existing toolset for automation cannot provide the detail on SUT behavior that Hierarchical Steps does.

The remainder of MetaAutomation therefore functions as motivation for making the big change with Hierarchical

Steps and Atomic Check, starting with download, run, inspect and modification of any of the sample implementations provided.

The Name "MetaAutomation" and the Whole

"Meta" is self-referential.

Think of the "Meta" of MetaAutomation as addressing the topic of quality automation at a higher level than before, answering the question "Why are we driving the product with repeatable automation, and how can the business best benefit?" with clarity and insight to open a new level of productivity. More precisely, the "Meta" could relate to the three paradigm shifts (pages 37-38): the first paradigm shift involving the change to use a system that is fully capable of persisting behavior and performance information from the product, the second paradigm shift about including the full scope of what automation can do for quality measurement and communication around the larger team that includes both dev and QA, and the third paradigm shift that requires looking at the whole SUT including the ecosystem, if possible.

See the The MetaAutomation pattern map on page 73.

The Need for a Pattern Language

As Nikos Salingaros wrote in the introduction to his 2000 paper,

> *The language of a group of patterns forms the groundwork for any discipline. (Salingaros 2000)*

There is a lot of skill and ability represented in my field of software quality, but there has not yet been an attempt to describe the entire problem space as seen in the The MetaAutomation pattern map on page 73.

Christopher Alexander inspired patterns in software, from his work in architecture. He wrote in "The Timeless Way of Building"

> *It is only because a person has a pattern language in his mind, that he can be creative when he builds. (Alexander 1979, p.206)*

Alexander follows with clarification: good rules can be liberating, rather than constricting, because they point the way towards understanding and delivering value.

The nine patterns of MetaAutomation are more than a list or a catalog; they form a structure with defined dependencies, and together they define a whole, a coherent solution to a problem space I call "quality automation:" how best to drive automated measurements of functional and performance software quality and communicate the quality to stakeholders of the business, both human and automated processes, fast and often. With quality automation, the quality measurements, recording, re-measuring, directing, and presenting communication are all potentially automated, working from the least dependent patterns up as they make sense for the software developing organization. The more dependent patterns form a strong, clear expression of business value to motivate implementing the less dependent patterns (Leszak et al. 2000).

Common misunderstandings and practices around software quality are preventing software from achieving levels of quality that are necessary today, and crucial tomorrow. Current, pervasive, and very costly misunderstandings include the persistent but obsolete meme that "The point of test is to find bugs" (Myers 1979).[82] There is also commonly a poor understanding, or even a complete discounting, of the fact that automated verifications can excel in a very different business value than what manual testing offers.

Traditional yet limiting practices include using the Linear Logging antipattern. This appears as linearly occurring log statements with inherently weak contextual information, in procedures of automated verifications where context is actually very important. Logs work great for isolated events (e.g., with web servers), but they are very poor for conveying context of a step in a procedure. The result: after a check has run, whether it passed or failed, there is

little information on what the SUT did during the check. Going to source code to find out is difficult and imprecise.

MetaAutomation solves the problems of misguided design and lost information for automated quality measurement and communication.

As a pattern language, MetaAutomation clarifies the nature and boundaries of the quality automation problem space for the software business and clarifies how teams might implement solutions. It highlights the benefits of taking an enlightened, creative approach to quality automation rather than the historical limitations of current practices.

The Name "MetaAutomation"

The "Meta" of MetaAutomation invites a broadening of perspective, a more abstract, general, and high-level view of applying automation to software quality. It begins by asking the question: if we do apply automation to software quality, what can we learn from first principles and the big-picture view to deliver the greatest quality-management value to ship software faster and at lower risk?

---

[82] See the section "The Tyranny of Bugs" on pages 16-18.

Fig. 15. MetaAutomation enables faster software development at lower quality risk.

Overview

The pattern map in Figure 16 opposite shows the 9 patterns of MetaAutomation, their names and grouping to clarify the function of each of the patterns in the larger pattern language context, and the problem space bounds – the interfaces with the business and the software under development. An arrow from one pattern to a second one shows that the second pattern depends on either the concepts or an implementation of the first.

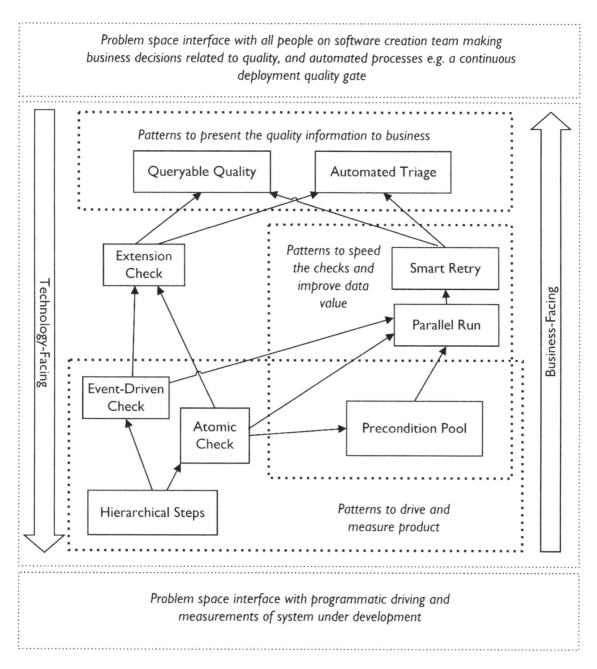

Fig. 16. The MetaAutomation pattern map.

At the bottom of Figure 16 is the technology-facing context. This is how MetaAutomation relates to the code of the system under development, technological dependencies that the product has, and/or technologies used to drive the system for quality purposes.

At the top of Figure 16 is the business-facing context: people on the team making business decisions related to quality, and any automated processes outside of quality that drive the business, e.g., promoting a system build as part of software continuous deployment.

Note that this book presents the pattern "Prioritized Requirements" because it is essential to effective quality automation. However, the scope of requirements is much larger than the scope of quality automation, so it is not part of the MetaAutomation pattern language.

The following table summarizes the patterns of MetaAutomation as presented in this book.

Pattern Name	Problem	Solution
Hierarchical Steps	How to record all interaction details with the SUT to support query and analysis?	SUT-driving code to create at runtime an extensible hierarchy, like XML.
Atomic Check	How to maximize the value, trustworthiness, speed, and scalability of quality data?	Make each check independent and drive the SUT to verify one requirement or requirement cluster per check.
Event-Driven Check	Events drive the SUT, internally and externally. How to get fast, repeatable, trustworthy measurements of functional quality?	The SUT subscribes to external events from the automation. Verifications wait on events as needed.
Extension Check	How can the team get fast and trustworthy feedback on quality issues that cannot be driven deterministically?	Instrument or measure the SUT on the non-deterministic quality aspect and store the data in the artifact of another check. Run verification(s) on the data created by the first check.
Precondition Pool	Is there a way to boost check performance, make checks more reliable, and improve check run data?	Actively manage preconditions out-of-line in a pool or pools.

Parallel Run	How can the business run many checks quickly, to scale with available computing resources?	Distribute runs of the individual checks across (virtual) machines or environments.
Smart Retry	How can automation *not* interrupt team members with false positives and check failures that need reproducing?	For configured root causes of a fail, immediately retry the check for a total of 2-3 tries, and group resulting data.
Automated Triage	How can automation direct notifications of check failures to select responsible individuals, rather than everybody?	Send actionable notifications only to those who would act.
Queryable Quality	What does the team need to get queryable and interactive role-appropriate views, not just of check results, but of detailed SUT behavior and performance as well?	Create a link-able, query-able interactive portal to show the data, starting with business-facing details and allowing drill-down to technology-facing details.

As Alexander wrote in his book "A Pattern Language: Towns, Buildings, Construction"

> *A pattern language has the structure of a network… However, when we use the network of a language, we use it as a sequence…"* (Alexander 1977, p.xviii)

So, this book presents the pattern language MetaAutomation starting with the Hierarchical Steps and Atomic Check patterns, just as the working software samples do.[83]

Pattern Form

This book presents the patterns in a generic form:

1. Pattern name
2. Summary
3. Context
4. Problem
5. Forces
6. Solution
7. Resulting Context
8. Examples

The *pattern name* is short, descriptive, and memorable.

---

[83] See the working samples on pages 161-176.

The *summary* is an overview of what the pattern is about and how it is useful.

The *context* lays the groundwork for the problem and keeps the pattern focused. It includes answers to these questions: What is going on around the problem? What defines the scope of the problem? (Harrison 1999)

The *problem* describes what is most visible about what is wrong when the pattern is not used, that would be resolved if the pattern were applied. What problem(s) does this pattern solve?

Forces define the problem by describing things that make the problem important, difficult, or scary, and what motivates a solution to the problem.

The *solution* solves the problem in a compelling way.

Resulting context is the context, again, but after the pattern is applied. What are the upsides and downsides of applying the pattern?

Examples ground the pattern in the real world. The examples should relate to your professional knowledge and experience.[84]

Running Example

To help illustrate each pattern, I use a running example: BankingAds, a hypothetical bank portal web app.

BankingAds enables a bank customer to make deposits, pay bills, withdraw from loans, make transfers between accounts and any other common banking operation, from any modern web browser. Advertisements appear to the side of the screen from an external advertising company. The differentiator for BankingAds is that (carefully anonymized) information from the end-user's account balance, activities, and history, feed the decision engine which leads to showing certain advertisements. The ads arrive asynchronously but may be based on what the end-user is doing at the time.

The team that creates and maintains BankingAds includes the QA or "Quality Assurance" role, that measures and supports quality and helps the team develop the software faster. Each pattern includes an example of how the people of this role apply the pattern during their work with the BankingAds project.

Review Questions

The answers are on page 208.

1) What makes MetaAutomation a pattern language, rather than just a set of design patterns?
2) What is the least-dependent, starting pattern for MetaAutomation?
3) What is the relationship between quality automation and MetaAutomation?

---

[84] If the examples do not relate to your professional knowledge and/or experience, or they could do better, please engage and give feedback through the LinkedIn™ group "Quality Automation" described on pages 159-160.

Chapter 9
Software Pattern: Prioritized Requirements

Summary

The Prioritized Requirements pattern is about discussing, discovering, recording, and prioritizing the implementation-independent business requirements for a software project, then using them to link to and prioritize the functional requirements as those are developed. The functional requirements are measurable with automation. For the scope of this book, functional requirements are the same as system requirements.

Fig. 17. People meet to gather and prioritize requirements.

As Goldsmith writes

> *Organizations that learn to identify business requirements well can gain an insurmountable advantage over competitors that persist in getting conventional results with conventional approaches... Recently, the heads of both IBM and Hewlett-Packard have announced independently that success today in the information systems industry demands primary attention to understanding the needs of the customer, in other words, the business' requirements. (Goldsmith 2004, p.xx)*

Prioritized Requirements is not part of the MetaAutomation pattern language or the pattern map on page 73. It is both business-facing for business requirements *and* technology-facing for functional requirements, but the pattern does not include implementation in the quality automation problem space. This book includes it for clarity and to emphasize the importance to the patterns in MetaAutomation that depend on it: The Precondition Pool pattern, and all the "Check" patterns.

Context

The context is creating software, especially software that matters to people.

When creating software, requirements inform what the team builds, how, and for whom. Requirements also inform relative priority of different things the SUT does or will do, which does not necessarily map to feature implementation order but can help with prioritizing behavior verifications and bug searches.

Problem

For a team of people building software, there must be clarity and consensus on the requirements. Also, the team must prioritize requirements for both implementation and behavioral verifications.

As Elisabeth Hendrickson wrote,

Knowing the requirements for a system means understanding the problem to be solved. If the problem isn't understood, the solution can't address it. Not taking time for requirements discovery at the beginning will cost far more time and money in the end. (Hendrickson 2003)

To make the case for getting the requirements as correct as possible given current team knowledge, Robin Goldsmith notes

… the cost of fixing an error rises by a factor of about 10 for each additional stage at which the error is fixed. (Goldsmith 2004, p.9)[85]

Insufficient clarify and consensus on requirements creates project and quality risk. For software that matters to people, the risk is significant.

The Agile software development movement has some wonderful things going for it, but when the Agile Manifesto explicitly values

Individuals and interactions over processes and tools

Working software over comprehensive documentation

Customer collaboration over contract negotiation

---

[85] On this point Goldsmith also cites Barry Boehm's 1981 book "Software Engineering Economics."

Responding to change over following a plan (Agile Manifesto)

It almost begs software teams to avoid any supportive structures to their software creation, e.g., written requirements. The manifesto is often interpreted that way. This works for software that has negligible impact on people's lives, but not for software that matters.

Teams often put too little emphasis on creating, discovering, recording, and prioritizing requirements. This can unintentionally create risks related to ambiguity, including lack of clarity or consensus, on what the team expects the SUT to do. It can also diminish robustness if there are personnel changes on the team. Priority inversion – where the team is working on some part of the SUT but deferring until later some aspect which (with greater clarity) would be higher priority – can create quality and project risk as well. There also can be confusion about progress or when the product is ready.

To the extent that requirements for the project are not known, there is no clarity about what the software is meant to do or for whom. The result is confusion, wasted effort and cost, and poor communication within the team. There is also risk of team turnover: if there is so much unwritten knowledge with one team member that this person is pivotal to project success, and that person leaves for some reason, it will be difficult and expensive (if possible at all) to get the team back on track with the project.

Requirements can change, but if requirements change from an unknown state, the earlier state of requirements and/or the rationale for those requirements might be unknown. Earlier decisions, or the reasons for those decisions, become lost information. If that lost information is still important for the project, the project might drift away unintentionally, creating quality and project risk.

To expose lack of requirements, one might ask: "Why does the software do this (specific thing)?" If the answer is as vague as "the team is going this direction" or "my boss told me to" then there might be no requirements to give supportive structure to the effort.

Teams sometimes track functional requirements, but not business requirements. Not knowing the business requirements creates quality risk when functional requirements change. This quality risk can take the form of something called "requirements creep" and it is realized when the team (or worse, the end-user) learns that part of the system is built wrong. As Goldsmith notes

> *By learning to better identify the real, business requirements, we can dramatically reduce the requirements creep that many people think is inevitable. (Goldsmith 2004, p.40)*

Forces

It is easier, in the short term, to not write anything down. Discovering, discussing, recording, reviewing, and sometimes maintaining or changing requirements takes time and effort.

The team needs to know what it is building, why, and for whom. This need is acute for complex or high-impact projects and large or distributed teams.

The team needs requirements to guide design as well.

Good requirements show developers exactly what to develop, and they help in prioritizing work items for developers.

Requirements with correct priority are essential for behavior verifications, as with quality automation, and in looking for bugs.

The team needs prioritized requirements to prioritize bugs and any resulting work items for the team.

Solution

At or near project start, discuss, discover, record, and prioritize business requirements. As much as you can, make your business requirements independent of design and implementation.

When designing a solution from business requirements, functional requirements become clear. Record those and link to business requirements. Business requirements and functional requirements link together in many-to-many relationships, so the team might implement a business requirement with software that fulfills one or more functional requirements, and a functional requirement might relate to one or more business requirements.

Use the business requirement priority to prioritize the functional requirements.

When business requirements change during the project, the new or changed functional requirements and their priority become clear by association with new, changed, and existing business requirements.

Agile software development emphasizes iterative development, with little ceremony and documentation. The Agile Manifesto states as a principle,

> *Welcome changing requirements, even late in development. Agile processes harness change for the customer's competitive advantage. (Agile Manifesto)*

It is important for software creators to know that welcoming "changing requirements" does not negate the value of finding and recording more of the requirements in the first place, however. As Goldsmith notes

> *In my experience, iterative development is far more productive and satisfying when it begins with identifying the real requirements. I've found that defining real requirements well not only takes no longer overall to create systems, it actually takes much less time than the illusory iterating based on system requirements alone. (Goldsmith 2004, p.48)*

Discovering, defining and (in precise, succinct language) recording business requirements mitigates risk and helps the team communicate and build the right thing, even in the likelihood of requirements additions or changes in future. Linking clearly known requirements to design decisions and quality automation increases agility because the scope of changes is transparent to anyone on the team; fewer meetings and discussions are needed to verify what was intended.

As Goldsmith writes,

> *The format that I've found most suitable for documenting business requirements is a hierarchical list of itemized business deliverable "whats" that contribute to value when delivered.* (Goldsmith 2004, p.155)

The business requirements, i.e., the business deliverable *whats* that Goldsmith describes, must be itemized for traceability in the software development process.

User stories can be useful in creating dialogue with customers and discovering business requirements, but there is risk in mistaking them for business requirements because they often have implementation-specific information and vague rationale expressed in user vernacular. They are also often not as granular as itemized business requirements must be. The team can avoid these problems with carefully written user stories.

It is difficult or even impossible to record *all* requirements, especially business requirements, because the scope is open-ended. It is low-risk to leave the very large-scope or very small-scope requirements implicit.

For more on requirements, please see Goldsmith's book in the references at the back of this book.

Resulting Context

The result of applying this pattern is business requirements for the project are described and prioritized. They might be in a list, or a hierarchy.

The functional requirements are complete enough to guide design, implementation, and quality efforts. They link to the business requirements, either in one-to-one relationships or many-to-many.

If business requirements change, the scope of the downstream changes, and the relative priority, become clear in terms of end-user impact.

If functional requirements change, the relative priority of the changes follow from their relationships to the business requirements.

Examples

Example: BankingAds

For the BankingAds project, the team interviews potential clients and otherwise does some market research for what people say they want. Next, they use this information to create and prioritize a set of implementation-independent business requirements that meets those needs and differentiates their product in the way they want.

For example,

1. login must be easy
2. Balances shown must always be up-to-the-moment correct
3. transfers must be easy and quick

Etc.

These might be prioritized in decreasing priority order: 2, 1, and 3. For example, correct balances are more important than easy login because the potential impact of failure is greater.

Then, on to functional requirements. The functional requirements are linked to business requirements and so prioritized by association. Functional requirements are measurable by automation.

Now, as requirements and design progress, the team learns what it is building. Functional requirements become the root for what the QA role needs to verify and communicate, starting with the Hierarchical Steps and Atomic Check patterns.[86]

Review Questions

The answers are on pages 208-209.

1) List two reasons that business requirements are important in addition to functional requirements.
2) What are some risks to the product of not knowing business requirements?

---

[86] More on how requirements relate to MetaAutomation is on pages 28-29.

Chapter 10
MetaAutomation Pattern: Hierarchical Steps

Summary

This pattern is about using an ordered-tree hierarchy to think about, remember, record, and/or communicate a repeatable procedure.

Fig. 18. The hierarchy of steps for a journey: the house destination as root step of the hierarchy, tents as child steps of house, stones as child steps of tents, and the robot's footsteps as child steps of the stones.

Context

In the world of people doing things, people usually have plans and intentions for their actions. People achieve many things with multiple steps.

People often need to remember, communicate, record, and/or follow the steps.

Problem

Multi-step procedures towards some goal are universal to the human experience. Effective expression, persistence, or communication of such procedures is widespread but not universal. The quality automation problem domain is a good illustration of this problem because of the need for detailed records of procedures which are — most often — repeated exactly.

Conventional practices of using automation to drive the SUT to measure and communicate software quality suffer from poor practice. Log statements, exceptions, or even implemented keywords are better than nothing at granting clarity into what automation drives the SUT to do, but they lack detail, context, fidelity, and trustworthiness.

When driving the SUT for quality measurements, the details of interacting with the SUT are as important as the ultimate measurement results (Davies et al. 2014). This is true whether a check passes or fails. Both types of information are valuable to the business (Parveen et al. 2007). Together, if persisted and handled efficiently, they can help the rest of the quality automation process reach much greater speed and efficiency and become more effective at ensuring that quality always moves forward.

More precisely, knowledge of how automation drives the SUT can prevent

- False positives
- false negatives
- low trust
- poor communication about SUT behavior, especially across teams, roles, and geographies
- re-work by people doing manual testing in coordination with the automation.

Without those details, for the team to ensure that quality is always moving forward is difficult and expensive if it is possible at all (Herzig and Nagappan 2015) (Jiang et al. 2017) (Elbaum et al. 2014).

Unfortunately, conventional practices that rely on scattered log statements in non-shipping automation code are very lossy and therefore poorly suited to recording how automation drives and measures the SUT, especially if more quality automation consumes the artifacts from the check runs.[87] Such practices lose most of the business value of the data.

Forces

- For casual expression of a procedure, an ordered list of steps appears simpler.
- In the quality automation problem domain, automation must persist the details of how it drives and measures the SUT,

---

[87] The more-dependent patterns of MetaAutomation all do powerful things with the artifacts, but the record of what happened

must be complete, as they are with the Hierarchical Steps and Atomic Check patterns.

with a structure that supports later reporting and analysis.

- Logs are a powerful tool from a different problem domain, but by nature each log statement is persisted in isolation from all the others, thereby losing important contextual information.
- Performance of non-shipping automation code is not as critical as with product code.
- Hierarchical Steps are more complex to implement than log statements.
- Steps naturally form an ordered tree when some steps are at a higher level of abstraction than other steps, and other steps are at a finer level of detail.

Solution

In non-shipping automation code, record in a hierarchy all the information of how code drives and measures the SUT and how the SUT responds. XML supports this well, as shown in running sample code, free for reuse or modification.[88]

The hierarchy nodes need names.[89] To support readability, query and analysis, and other automated operations with the data, the names must be stable. The samples (pages 161-176) show a straightforward way to do this with hard-coded strings and show how data can be added in data nodes, as needed, in the generated structures.

All the details of a check are now persisted and available with context information. They are in a form that is suitable to efficient and reliable automated analysis. For the business, the hierarchy presents the business-facing details at and near the root of the hierarchy, and the technology-facing details at and near the leaf nodes of the hierarchy. The names closer to the root of the hierarchy can be a business-friendly language, also called the "ubiquitous" language of the domain experts, while the names closer to the leaf nodes can be more a brief functional description of the step.[90]

---

[88] See the section "How to Use the Samples" on pages 163-166.

[89] As implemented in the samples in XML, these are specifically elements, i.e., the element type of node.

[90] Popularized with the 2003 book "Domain-Driven Design" by Eric Evans, and nicely described in the 2008 "The Art of Agile Development" by Shore and Warden.

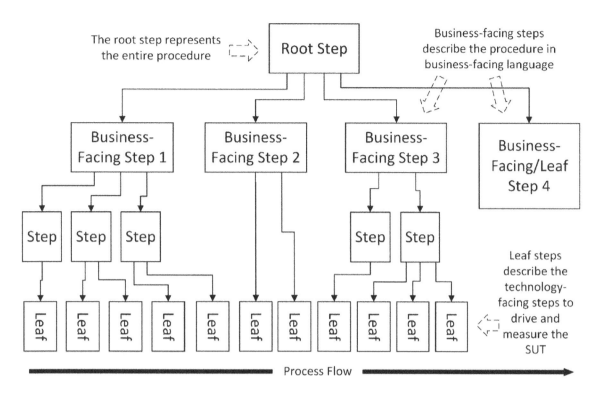

Fig. 19. The hierarchy of steps for a procedure.

Implementing code to create a hierarchy at runtime from the nested steps of a check is challenging, but the samples do it for you with open source (see introduction).

A check failure propagates up the hierarchy from the leaf step where the error occurred to the root step, where the step name describes the entire check. If the same check has run before successfully, the record from the earlier check run shows all the steps, so it is clear by comparison which steps were blocked. Blocked steps show quality risk, because they show quality that might be unknown due to the earlier failure.

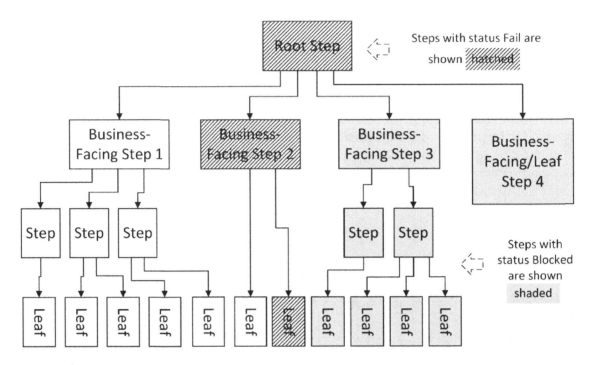

Fig. 20. A failure in a procedure represented in a hierarchy.

Adding or removing steps has a limited effect on the hierarchy, and therefore a limited effect on existing data. This in turn improves the value of check data over time for extended analysis.

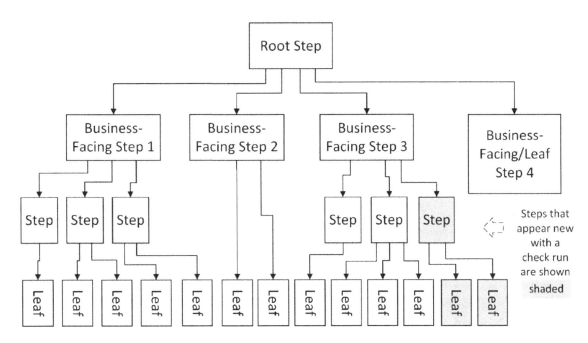

Fig. 21. Adding steps to a procedure represented as a hierarchy.

Figure 21 above shows the limited impact of adding steps to a hierarchical view of a procedure.

Resulting Context

Expression of a procedure is complete, extensible with more detail, changeable with limited impact, and very descriptive for failures.

All these benefits carry over to driving the SUT with automation. With the self-documenting automation code shown in the samples, this gives unprecedented clarity into what the automation code is doing (Collins and Lucena Jr. 2012).

The artifact of a check includes every detail. Every step has an explicit relationship to other steps, including peer steps, steps at a higher level of abstraction (oriented towards the business) and lower levels of abstraction (towards the technology, i.e., driving the product).

Since the artifact of the run of a check is in XML, it supports robust and performant analysis.

These aspects support the Queryable Quality pattern[91] of MetaAutomation:

- The business-facing orientation of the root node of the hierarchy
- The technology-facing process of drilling down to the leaf nodes of the SUT-driving steps and measurements

---

[91] See the Queryable Quality pattern on pages 155-158.

This detailed knowledge of the root cause of failure for a check support the Smart Retry[92] and Automated Triage[93] patterns. For example, as shown above in Figure 20, an error that fails the check propagates up through the hierarchy to the root node. All levels of the hierarchy show, in their respective contexts, where the check failed.

Examples

Example: The Composite pattern

The intent of the Composite pattern:

> *Compose objects into tree structures to represent part-whole hierarchies. Composite lets clients treat individual objects and compositions of objects uniformly. (Gamma 1995)*

This is a useful technique in computer code, and I applied in in the samples referenced in MetaAutomation.net to represent hierarchies in both observations and executions of procedures.[94]

Example: installing a dishwasher

A hierarchy of steps is a natural way to express a procedure to install a dishwasher in your home. If "Installing the Dishwasher" were the root node of a hierarchy, the child nodes would include "Remove the old one," "clean the space," "supply electrical power," "hook up water supply," "hook up drain," and "test dishwasher and installation." Each of those nodes has many more details as well, which, with a hierarchy, can go into child nodes. This has the advantages of making the installation instructions easier to follow and work-arounds easier to find should some part of the procedure fail or be inapplicable to the specific installation, as compared to the case of the procedure expressed as a (potentially very long) linear list of steps.

---

[92] See the Smart Retry pattern on pages 141-150.
[93] See the Automated Triage pattern on pages 151-154.

[94] The samples are on pages 161-176.

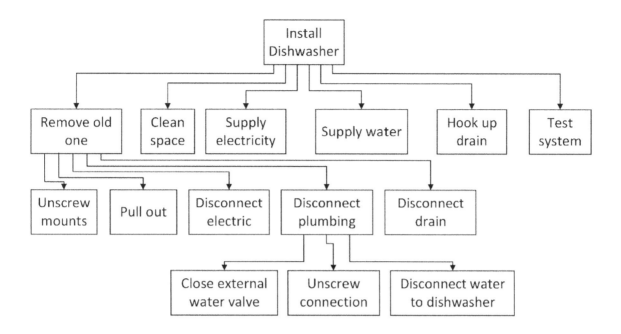

Fig. 22. Incomplete hierarchy of steps for installing dishwasher.

This step hierarchy diagram is very incomplete because listing more steps in the hierarchy would take more space than is available here.

Example: cooking with a recipe

A hierarchy of steps expresses a complex recipe, for similar reasons.

Example: business task

Suzanne Sebillotte describes how a hierarchy is a best expression of steps to achieve a task, as this graphic from her paper shows (Sebillotte 1988) (Figure 23):

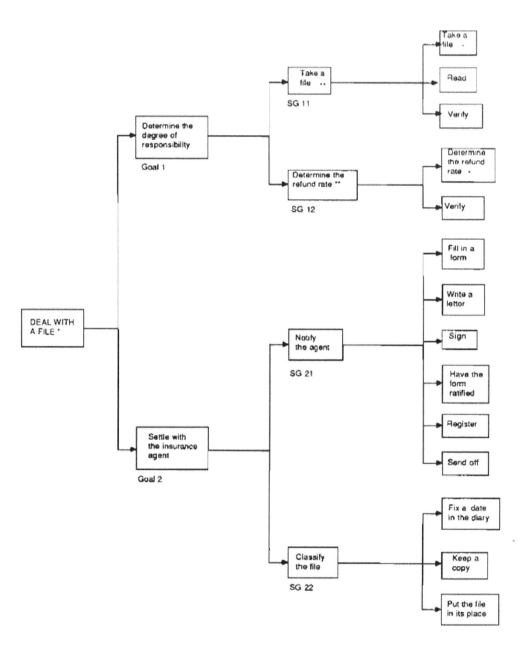

Fig. 23. The task hierarchy of Sebillotte.

Hierarchical task analysis does not assume that the order of steps is always the same or completed sequentially. However, the Hierarchical Steps pattern describes procedures or parts of procedures where the order is stable, and either inherently sequential, or managed with thread synchronization to become sequential. This is necessary for quick and reliable quality measurements. The promise of MetaAutomation, to enable faster and more confident software development, depends on such measurements.

For example, given the GUI of an app, there are usually at least several different approaches towards achieving a given task. Automation measures each with a separate check. Each such check would have a distinct but stable hierarchy.

Example: pre-flight

Figure 24 below shows a graphic from the owner's manual for a 1967 Cessna 172/Skyhawk. This is a nice visual example of how the Hierarchical Steps pattern occurs naturally, with the station steps (1-6) around the airplane standing for a higher level in the hierarchy and the lettered steps at each station standing for the lower level, i.e., child steps of the station steps (Cessna 1984).

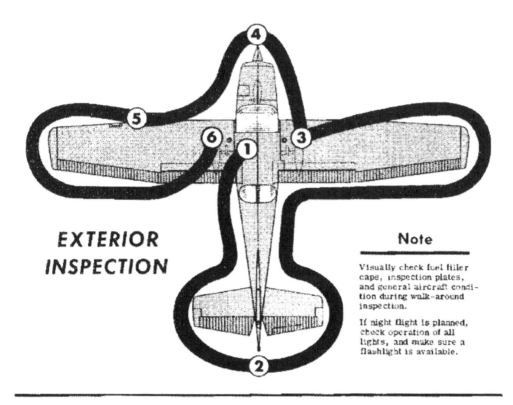

EXTERIOR INSPECTION

Note

Visually check fuel filler caps, inspection plates, and general aircraft condition during walk-around inspection.

If night flight is planned, check operation of all lights, and make sure a flashlight is available.

 a. Turn on master switch and check fuel quantity indicators, then turn master switch off.
b. Check ignition switch "OFF".
c. Check fuel selector valve handle "BOTH ON."
d. On first flight of day and after each fueling, pull out strainer drain knob for about four seconds, to clear fuel strainer of possible water and sediment.
e. Remove control wheel lock.
f. Check baggage door for security.

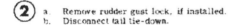 a. Check oil level. Do not operate with less than six quarts. Fill for extended flight.
b. Check propeller and spinner for nicks and security.
c. Check nose wheel strut and tire for proper inflation.
d. Disconnect tie-down rope.
e. Make visual check to insure that fuel strainer drain valve is closed after draining operation.

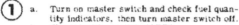 a. Remove rudder gust lock, if installed.
b. Disconnect tail tie-down.

 a. Remove pitot tube cover, if installed, and check pitot tube opening for stoppage.
b. Check fuel tank vent opening for stoppage.
c. Check stall warning vent opening for stoppage.

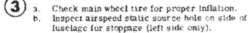 a. Check main wheel tire for proper inflation.
b. Inspect airspeed static source hole on side of fuselage for stoppage (left side only).
c. Disconnect wing tie-down.

 Same as .

Fig. 24. Hierarchical steps of preflight for a small airplane.

Example: buying a plane ticket

In the domain of running software, a good example is buying a plane ticket online. Web pages and controls on the pages arrange the steps of the ticket-buying experience. The itinerary request occurs on one page, where the traveler enters origin and destination, one-way vs. round trip, leave and return dates etc. The leave and return dates include month, day, and year. This naturally forms a hierarchy: the root node is the overall task of buying a plane ticket. The children of the root are each of the web pages that hold information and choices for the passenger to make. Child nodes of the page nodes include items such as name and date. The name node includes first, middle, and last names. The date nodes include month, day, and year. This hierarchical arrangement leads the purchaser through a process where the context is clear for each step. This clarity and ease-of-use would be impossible if the steps were a long linear list of ordered items to read or enter information.

Example: BankingAds

For the BankingAds running example, suppose the root of the hierarchy was the overall operation of the check "Transfer $5 from savings into checking," and the verification cluster[95] included before and after balances for savings and checking for the transferred amount. The root step "Transfer $5 from savings into checking" might have three child steps:

1. Login
2. make the transfer
3. log out

The login step has five child steps

1. load the login page
2. verify it is the correct page
3. enter credentials
4. initiate login (e.g., with a login button)
5. verify that login was successful

The "enter credentials" step has two child steps:

1. enter user name
2. enter password

Suppose the "enter user name" step fails due to a bug on the page: the field is read-only. The error propagates up to the "enter credentials" step, which propagates up to the "login" step, which propagates up to the root step "Transfer $5 from savings into checking." The check has failed, and the nature of the failure is clear and available for rich analysis at all the levels of abstraction. The root cause of failure is clear with the failed leaf step — "enter user name" — and the exception that is caught by the check code and packaged in the result of the check.

The Hierarchical Steps pattern, applied to automation, records in full detail driving and measuring the SUT. Each step shows context by position in the hierarchy and the record shows how many milliseconds each step took. In case of check fail, the result

---

[95] More discussion on verification clusters on pages 104-105.

shows cause of failure at all hierarchy levels and all blocked steps.

This saves enormous amounts of debugging time, makes separate development of performance tests unnecessary, and communicates what BankingAds is doing correctly (or not) with performance information. Hierarchical Steps enables drill-down from the highest level of abstraction down to the atomic steps of driving the product, thereby making the information available to anyone on the team concerned with product quality.

Review Questions

The answers are on pages 209-210.

1) Find an example of how the Hierarchical Steps pattern could describe something you did today.
2) What is an essential difference between ideal applications for logs and automated driving of the SUT for quality measurements?
3) XML is not part of the Hierarchical Steps pattern. Why is it an ideal metalanguage for computing with Hierarchical Steps?

Chapter 11
MetaAutomation Pattern: Atomic Check

Summary

Atomic Check is about a simple, independent, focused automated procedure to verify a functional requirement and record detailed data on interacting with the SUT (Kappler 2016).

This pattern — or, at least part of it — is used widely. Effective practitioners in the field use simple, focused checks, per recommendations of Adam Goucher:

> "…This rule is states that a test case should only be measuring one, and only one thing."[96]

"*Test cases should not be dependent on other test cases.*" *(Goucher 2008)*

As Meszaros writes,

> *We should avoid the temptation to test as much functionality as possible in a single Test… it is preferable to have many small Single-Condition Tests… (Meszaros 2007, p. 359).*

---

[96] The grammatical error is in the original, but the meaning is clear.

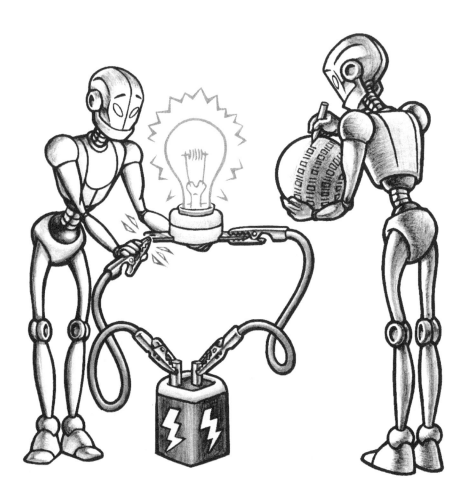

Fig. 25. Automation performing a check and recording detailed results.

Context

- The Hierarchical Steps[97] pattern, applied to quality automation, enables complete and trustworthy data in a robust hierarchical structure.
- Applying the Prioritized Requirements[98] pattern ensures that most of the functional requirements are known, and most of those are measurable with automation.
- Automation for fast verification of SUT builds, data, or code change sets, must drive and measure the SUT with repeatable checks.
- Automation persists all that data in the check result, along with pass/fail results.
- Given a large number of checks that need to be run often, scale with resources is important.

Problem

With conventional practices, the business loses valuable quality data. This happens in many ways, including

- Early failures in a long and complex check block quality data or make it untrustworthy.
- Quality data is too expensive because the checks take a very long time to run.
- In case of check pass, the team disregards what a check does to the SUT, in part due to the enduring misconception that test is only about finding bugs.

Risks to the software business include

- The checks become expensive on failure because the team needs a manual debugging session to find root cause if they can reproduce the failure at all.
- If the team runs quality automation with stubbed-out or faked services that the SUT uses, that automation is not testing the entire SUT as end-users would experience it. Service changes or failures can be very high-risk events, and not verifying early and often how the SUT handles these creates significant unnecessary risk; there might be rude surprises at integration time.
- If the team relies too much on checks that are not repeatable, too many failures are inconsistent or difficult to reproduce. Code in a shared repository might get corrupted with flaws that might otherwise be kept out.

---

[97] See the Hierarchical Steps on pages 85-98.

[98] See the Prioritized Requirements on pages 77-83.

There is also the challenge described in Huizinga and Kolowa's 2007 book *Automated Defect Prevention*:

> *"The (regression automation) should be configured to provide sufficient detail for an architect or developer to review the regression report and be able to investigate the problem without having to run any additional tests.... The (regression automation) should provide ... information ... to identify the location and the cause of the regression. (Huizinga and Kolowa 2007, p.289)*

How does one design a check to maximize the quality, quantity, and trustworthiness of data on the SUT, maximize the value of quality automation, and minimize quality risk?

Forces

- Computing power and resources used for the software development process, including quality management, are increasingly available and inexpensive.
- The team, especially software developers, must get detailed and trustworthy quality data quickly and reliably.
- A complex SUT needs many checks to verify that it meets functional requirements.
- For a check to be appropriately prioritized and informative, it must be traceable to functional requirements (and business requirements).

Solution

Design and implement checks to be atomic —as simple as possible — given that:

- Each one must have a single target verification or verification cluster, linked to functional requirements.[99]
- Each must run with dependencies in place where possible.
- Each check must run completely independently of every other check.
- Each check must run (or, fail) as fast as possible.

Apply the Hierarchical Steps pattern to the steps of driving the product, and the measurements, so the check is self-documenting in an approachable and drill-able hierarchy.

The important aspect of simplicity for these checks is that there are as few points of failure as possible for a check that verifies a functional requirement. Adding more data to the artifact of this check, for example to support the Extension Check pattern on pages 125-128, does not conflict with Atomic Check if the check has no added points of failure as a result and does not take significantly longer.

---

[99] See the Prioritized Requirements pattern on pages 77-83.

Elements of the check

For speed, simplicity, robustness, and focus for the check, write it to ignore aspects of the SUT that are not needed for the target verification or verification cluster for that check. If there is something that goes unmeasured with this approach, then by the priority of the requirement that describes that aspect of SUT behavior, write another check to measure it.

Preliminary steps

Any in-line setup steps in the check are preliminary steps. These focus on getting to the check target by driving the SUT as simply as possible to meet the target. Extreme simplicity might appear to conflict with the independence of each check from every other check, but in that case the independence of the checks takes priority. See the section "Creating atomic checks from overlapping functional requirements" on pages 117-119.

Implicit verifications

Any preliminary step might also represent an implicit preliminary verification: implicit because no extra code is necessary, but verifications because a failure would fail the check by throwing some exception. The information included in any such exception is important for showing root cause of failure, from the point of view of driving the SUT, but it might not be adequate. Some preliminary steps need explicit verifications to fail sooner with good, actionable information, in case the state of the system means that the check is headed for failure.

Explicit verifications

If you have ever seen a check fail with a NullReferenceException (or something analogous), then you know that the team must follow up on such a message and decipher source code. In some cases of a more complex statement on that line of code, even knowing the source code line is not enough to make the check fail actionable. In either case, the value of automated handling of the failure, and the value to later viewing and analysis, will be limited by incomplete information at check fail.

In such cases where the check is headed for failure, the automation code needs explicit preliminary verifications to do two things:

1. Fail the check faster by detecting a failure case earlier
2. Fail the check with detailed and specific root cause information

See "Example: explicit preliminary check of User object" on pages 109-110 for a case where an explicit preliminary verification helps automation and the business.

For a working example, see the Sample 1 (pages 167-170) and Example 2 inside that sample. This example tests the web page built to fail randomly. Note where the check throws CheckFailException objects to give good, actionable information on root cause of the failure. These bits of code to throw the exception are explicit verifications because they are explicit in the code. Their purpose is to fail the check faster and give better information.

Target verification

The preliminary steps lead up to the check target. The check target links to a functional requirement and is the reason to have the check as part of the team's responsibility.

The target verification may include a step that interacts with the product, depending on the requirement, but never more than one step. More than one step in the target verification could lead to hiding or invalidating quality information in case there is a failure that blocks the final step that interacts with the product.

Verification cluster

Sometimes a check can verify two or more aspects of product behavior as a cluster in one check if there is no value to dividing the aspects between different checks. For example, several controls on a web page might be verified as a cluster, or several properties that are all required as part of an important operation.

Two verifications — call them A and B — cluster together as part of the target verification of a check if they meet all four of the following criteria:

1. Verifications A and B have similar importance to a functional requirement (or, to closely related requirements).

If a check could fail for either a fail in A, or B, or both, if one of them is much more important than the other, a fail of the check could cause a priority inversion: if the check causes a work item for a team

member, it could be handled as if it had a priority associated with A but actually the issue is B, or the opposite.

2. They are independent measurements, so A could happen either before or after B.

Suppose, for example, the functional requirement is that the initial state for a new user is "Active." A check verifies this requirement. The last three steps in sequence are a) get a reference to the user object b) verify that the user reference is not null c) verify that the status of this user is "Active." If either a) or b) fail, then c) is not defined and has no value; if either a) or b) fail, then c) is blocked.

If the check succeeds up to the point of the target verification, the target verification must be meaningful, for the generated data to be useful over the current check run and any future queries on the functional quality data set. The target verification can be "blocked," and that is meaningful, but in that case if steps a) and/or b) were included in the target verification, the results of those steps would be lost. Therefore, a) and b) must be outside the target verification for the check, as preliminary steps and/or verifications.

3. They link together logically.

Fails in A or B would cause similar actions, and if either or both A and B should fail, the state of the other property at check failure time is significant to the resulting action item.

4. Between the measurements of A and B, there is no interaction with the product or any external entity over the network.

The target verification links to a functional requirement (or, closely related requirements) and describes the reason for the check. Imagine some hypothetical target verification clusters:

I.   SUT-driving step
II. Verification step A
III. Verification step B

In this case, A and B are closely related and the results are both needed in case a check failure becomes an action item for the team. A and B could represent, for example, related properties of a web page or other results of a transaction with the SUT.

I.   Verification step A
II. Verification step B
III. Verification step C

Here, A, B, and C are closely related checks of some state, and relate to some functional requirement. If A, B, and C are of similar priority (or, importance) to the SUT, this works as a verification cluster.

But, consider this example:

I.   Verification step A
II. SUT-driving step
III. Verification step B

This does not work as a verification cluster because the SUT-driving step between verifications A and B could fail, and if that happens, either verification B cannot happen at all or it is invalidated because the SUT has entered an invalid (not designed) state. The verification step A might have valuable information for the check run that failed in the following step, but a smart retry might temporarily hide such information when the SUT-driving step does not fail in the retried check.[100]

If two criteria A and B meet all the four conditions listed above, then they can form a target verification cluster. With such a cluster, a failure for either A or B or both would fail the test, but in either case, A and B are both measured and included as strongly typed data points for the test run artifact. To be most useful at triage and analysis time, the artifact that results from check failure at the target verification needs the data and/or state of both A and B.

By extending these rules, a target verification cluster could have any number of verifications.

Steps

To ensure reliable and complete data on product behavior, have the check implementation document itself at runtime with an implementation of the Hierarchical Steps pattern, as the working samples do.

---

[100] The artifact from every check run is stored for potential later viewing or analysis, but the "temporary" hiding would happen because the retried check would be handled as a pass with no notification sent by the Automated Triage implementation.

Each step has a name. The name must be static to support queries and analyses that are based on that name.

For these steps, you can include as much added data as you want, but it must be structured to support automation, query, and analysis; see for example the method SetCustomDataCheckStep in the samples, and other methods of class Check.

Leaf steps – steps that do not have child steps – should have no more than one potential source of failure inside them. This is to ensure that, should the leaf step fail in a check, root cause from the perspective of the code driving the SUT is unambiguous.

Code

Coding style for quality automation is just as important as it is with product code, yet the optimal styles are quite different. Please see Appendix 3 on coding styles (pages 201-202) and the samples (pages 161-176) for more information.

Include all dependencies of the software environment, including services, to manage quality risk. Automation authors sometimes stub these out for speed and reliability, but patterns of MetaAutomation take care of those issues.[101] The best speed of a check run comes from applying the Atomic Check, Precondition Pool, and Parallel Run patterns. The Hierarchical Steps and Smart Retry patterns give reliability.

---

[101] For speed, see the Atomic Check, Precondition Pool, and Parallel Run patterns. For reliability, see the Hierarchical Steps, Atomic Check and Smart Retry patterns.

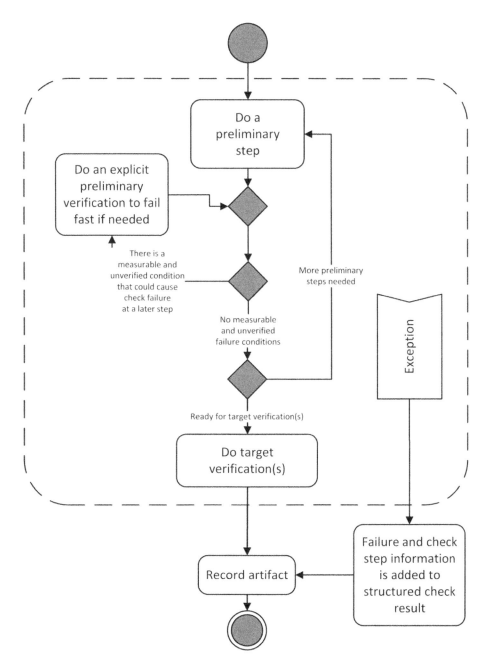

Fig. 26. The Atomic Check activity diagram.

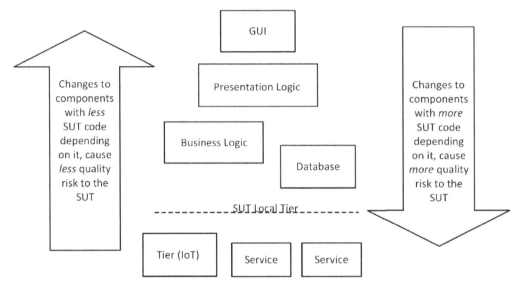

Fig. 27. Dependency vs. quality risk in a software system.

Figure 27 above shows the importance of including services and the less-dependent layers of the application for system testing.

Requirements give focus and priority

Atomic Check is about focusing the checks on what is important and what they are good at.

This means discovering and looking to requirements, not scenarios or stories, to know what to measure. Scenarios and stories can be helpful in discovering requirements, but as Goldsmith notes

> *Requirements need to be written.*
> *(Goldsmith 2004, p. 147)*

Please look to the Prioritized Requirements pattern on pages 77-83 for more on requirements and their importance.

Srivastva et al. wrote on prioritization

> *The objective ... is to develop a test case prioritization technique that prioritizes test cases on the basis of requirements that are more important than others, and risk factors that within a software project.*[102] *(Srivastva et al. 2008)*

Priority is important when verifying SUT behaviors because the most important behaviors must be verified especially quickly. That is what keep code breaks out of the shared repository – or, if the check-ins are not gated and the breaks make it in anyway, they are brought to light quickly while the team's knowledge of code changes is fresh.

---

[102] The grammatical error is in the original, but the meaning is clear.

Resulting Context

Simple verifications are faster and more trustworthy than complex ones. They give more focused product quality data as well and are simpler to link to functional requirements of the SUT.

The Atomic Check pattern helps the team by describing a standard and a procedure for defining an optimal check. This pattern, although detailed, is flexible and general enough that it applies to a wide variety of software products showing deterministic behavior and the deterministic foundations of probabilistic systems (e.g., machine learning software).

Checks that are each independent of other checks can run in any order and scale with computing resources.

Atomic Check supports Parallel Run[103] because the individual checks are all independent of each other, and fast and simple.

Atomic Check supports Smart Retry[104] and Automated Triage[105] with fast, simple, scalable checks, each with just one target verification or verification cluster, and detailed data joining all levels of the hierarchy and pointing at root cause of failure

For Queryable Quality,[106] all the check detail, for both passed and failed checks, is available. The business-facing root step of the check is central to check results, and drill-down is available to the leaf steps, that is, the technology-facing steps that drive and measure the SUT. This data is available to any team role or any distributed team around the world.

Examples

Example: explicit preliminary check of User object

If a preliminary step requires creating an object of type User, and if the User object creation might fail returning null, the check would fail by default at the attempt to do something with that User object. In this case, it would fail with a null reference exception or something analogous (depending on your programming language and framework). With only that information, this failure of the check could easily be ambiguous and therefore not actionable because root cause is not clear. Source code inspection by the owner of the automation might not resolve the ambiguity. This would need follow-up with a debug session by the check author or someone else on his/her team.

To implement the Atomic Check pattern and avoid the need for a QA-role debugging session in case of a failure of this type, this example needs at least one explicit preliminary verification. The check asserts (or uses equivalent test logic) that the User object is not null, with informative error information placed in the message to throw with the failure-case exception. The check can format dynamic information about the check run or failure into the

---

[103] See the Parallel Run on pages 135-140.
[104] See the Smart Retry on pages 141-150.

[105] See the Automated Triage on pages 151-154.
[106] See the Queryable Quality on pages 155-158.

exception message, where it will be included in the artifact of the check, but an even better technique is to create separate name/value pairs for the artifact, so that the data is more presentable and queryable. The samples of this book show this technique; look for the symbol SetCustomDataCheckStep in the code.

The check needs another preliminary verification if the User object has some property with a required value for the check to succeed. For example, if the check would fail later in case the User object is present but has a property that shows the user is not currently active, then there must be explicit verification for that property put in, with error information thrown with the exception.

Example: real estate web site

Suppose the SUT is a real estate web site, and you want to automate a check that verifies that search results on the public-facing site will show properties for sale.

The check has these steps:

1. Start a web browser with the URL of the site;
2. Click as needed to get to the property search page;
3. Change criteria as needed to get search results;
4. Verify that the resulting page shows at least one real estate property for sale.

When implementing this check, a developer needs much more detail to make all four steps occur. People are smart, but computers are not, so to get from the people-friendly four steps listed above to something that the automation can use, add some steps (in italics):

1. Start a web browser with the URL of the site;
2. Click as needed to get to the property search page *translates to*:
   a. Find the menu item on the page that shows the choices needed to proceed,
   b. Click the menu item,
   c. Find the "Property Search" submenu item,
   d. Click the submenu item,
   e. Wait for the Property Search page to load;
3. Change criteria as needed to get search results *translates to*:
   a. … (maybe nothing is needed to be done here);
4. Verify that the page shows at least one real estate property *translates to*:
   a. Find the HTML item that shows the number of properties that result from the query,
   b. Read the InnerText of that HTML item,
   c. Parse the text for the desired number,
   d. Assert that the number is greater than zero.

Any one of these steps could fail, due to check dependency failures, check code failures, or failures from the SUT.

Organizing the check into preliminary and target verifications is very simple for this example, because no two verifications meet all four of the clustering criteria above in the Target Verification section. Therefore, step 4d is the target verification for this check.

One of the goals of the Atomic Check pattern is to minimize the need for testers to follow up on a failed check with an intensive debug session just to answer the questions "What happened to cause the failure? Is this a test or a product bug, or something else?" Debug sessions on failed checks are very expensive and time-consuming, and as a result, they might not even happen at all. Even if they do happen, they cause delays and disorder for the team. The result is reduced value in the checks: they can still sometimes verify correct product behavior, but the team will tend to view failed checks as a test-owned failure rather than a product issue. It follows that the manual debug session that might turn a failed check into a fixed product bug is a barrier to the productivity of the team (as well as an obvious business cost).

Therefore, it is important to ensure that the artifacts from a failed check contain the information needed to know if someone needs to follow up, or at least maximize the chances that the artifacts are enough that the importance and impact (and potentially the resolution) of the failure is knowable, without a manual debug session.

Suppose, for example, that with our check on the real estate site, the check failed at step 4c: the parse failed for some reason. That the parse might fail *and* throw an exception makes it a preliminary verification for the check.

If this verification is left as implicit, on failure, one of several exception types is thrown. The exception has a stack trace that points to a file and line number in the source code, but the value of the string parsed is not reported to the artifact. This is valuable information to have at analysis and triage time, so make the verification explicit. Depending on language and environment, there are different approaches to solving this problem. A line of code doing an explicit null check might be an excellent choice, and something that in case of parse fail reports the value of the string that is the count of real estate properties on the web site.

Changes to make the verification explicit here help with manual triage, or smart retry, automated triage, or pattern detection through the Quality Portal or similar tool. For example, it might save the need for a debug session just to discover if the root cause of the failure is the web site, the framework, the test code, or some other dependency.

Suppose, for example, the text value discovered during the check run is "four," and that is consistent with design of the product. The failure to parse that string into an integer would then be a bug with the check code.

Suppose the text value parsed at step 4c is null or a zero-length string. That might be a significant and actionable product bug, and with the proper explicit preliminary verification, this is reported with the correct detail in the check artifact.

For this check on a real-estate web site, if step 4d – verifying that there is at least one property returned in the ultimate search – succeeds, then that is enough to pass the check. The end-user could continue in theory from that point with a further scenario because there is at least one property to look at. Step 4d is the target verification for the check.

This check needs explicit verifications so that enough information goes into the artifact associated with the failure, such that the results of the check are actionable. Another way of looking at this issue: when there are many check results and many failures, it is important that the check artifacts discriminate between the zero-length-string issue and the issue of the "four" case above.

Therefore, to cover the possibilities for steps 4b and 4c:

Add an explicit verification to step 4b requiring that the inner text of the HTML element returns a string that is non-null and with greater than zero length.

Add an explicit verification to step 4c so that if the parse should fail, the harness reports this as part of the check run artifact with the actual string. We need to know if the string that is expected to have the integer we want is "four" (which would be a check bug, if the product design allows for that kind of behavior for the SUT) or something else, like "1,0,01" (which would represent a product bug).

The target verification for the example is step 4d, by itself. Step 4d cannot succeed if any of the earlier steps fail, so by the second clustering criterion listed in the beginning of the Target verification section above, no clustering is needed.

Example: BankingAds

Returning to the BankingAds example, Atomic Check makes the checks

- traceable to functional requirements
- as fast as possible
- as scalable as possible
- as simple as possible
- as trustworthy as possible

and, the structure provided by the Hierarchical Steps pattern enables a single check to run across multiple deployment tiers and/or layers of the application, cross-process or cross-machine as needed, to assure quality for the Internet of Things. Sample 3 shows this.[107]

Bottom-up testing works well here, too: a check that drives and measures the application less the GUI or HTTP

---

[107] Sample 3 is on pages 173-176.

presentation, to verify balances, transfers, etc., will run much faster than if the GUI were included. If such a check fails, there is more detailed information from application code on root cause, and the failure is much closer to business logic, so resolution of the failure is quicker and more reliable. If such a check set passes and is followed by system checks that include the GUI, and there is a failure in the latter check set, based on comparing the checks, root cause is already known to be in the presentation code somewhere. Having different check sets that address well-understood layers of the application helps the team resolve the issue more quickly.

Example: REST service login

If we are testing a REST service for the ability of a certain account to log in, the focus of the check is successful login according to the criteria we specify, i.e., the message received and a given session cookie. The message and the cookie are both requirements for successful authentication. For this example, product components responsible for the message and/or the cookie are the responsibility of the product team.

The steps in that case include:

1. The client opening a network connection to the service;
2. The client creating, serializing, and sending an HTTP request;
3. The server successfully generating a response;
4. The response has a compatible HTTP status (200 OK);
5. The response body is successfully deserialized;
6. The response cookie is received, parsed, and stored.

The check includes verifications which might be implicit, that is, not directly expressed in the code. Check developers might choose to make the verifications explicit to ensure that in case of failure at a given step, the artifacts are informative enough to show root cause in the context of the check run. Supplementing the artifact with product data or other contextual information about driving the product might help to determine root cause. Product log data or instrumentation must be added to a distinct name/value pair in the artifact. Timing and scaling might be issues here because if there is data retrieved from the product and/or server, it must be synchronized.

The Atomic Check pattern still applies to this simple example, though, because the focus of the check is still one thing: successful authentication. Testing that one thing cannot be done in a simpler way or with fewer failure points.

This example gives a good look at a target verification cluster as well. Successful login depends on the HTTP status, the response body, and the response cookie. These three things all come with the same server response, so they can be measured together as a verification cluster: in case of check fail at verification, all three logically- and functionally-related aspects of behavior are measured and reported so they are available to the quality automation and to the business.

Example: creating an atomic check with persisted state in an application document

Consider a very simple document editing system.

Business requirements might include the following simple hierarchy, ordered by priority, highest-priority first:

1. User must create a persistent repository for information, and experience confirmation of this.
2. User must be able to make changes, and see the changes persist on the screen and in memory.
   a. Add text.
   b. Replace text.
   c. Delete text.
3. User must be able to search on text, and see results displayed.

Test cases for the system include various modifications of the document and points of verification to confirm operation success. For example, a manual test of this system that verifies the functional requirements might look like:

1. Create a document, and verify success;
2. Add some text, and verify that the text is added;
3. Replace some text, and verify correct result;
4. Search for text, and verify that search results are shown;

Automating this sequence would be creating a (non-atomic) check. It is important to keep in mind that the quality-measurement value of running the check manually is very different from running any automation of the same check steps. The team can then recognize the value of a person still running through the manual test or related scenarios occasionally.

People are smart and observant and can see many quality issues that a check would never bring to light. The value of the check is that for the automated points of verification of functional requirements, the verification can happen much faster and more reliably as part of the automation process. Any product quality regression is much easier to correct when found and reported quickly. If it is not found and communicated quickly it can cause more downstream costs and risks for the team, for example, cascading breaks or blocked scenarios.

The Atomic Check pattern is perfect for refactoring the above test into the best automation strategy for the feature. Steps 1-4 listed can be broken up into more than one check. The four steps described here sequentially as one check:

Step 1 → Step 2 → Step 3 → Step 4

Could be broken up into four atomic checks:

Check 1.   Step 1
        → Target Verification

Check 2.   Step 1 → Step 2
        → Target Verification

Check 3.   Step 1 → Step 2 → Step 3
        → Target Verification

Check 4.   Step 1 → Step 2 → Step 4
        → Target Verification

Each of these two tests does not depend on any other test, and that is a criterion of Atomic Check. This is progress because the tests are shorter and simpler.

Even the checks 3 and 4 listed here are more complex than they need to be. Suppose we use document images (e.g., through applying the Precondition Pool pattern on pages 129-134), and make a library of static images to use in our checks: DocumentA is an empty document, and DocumentB has some text in it already that will satisfy the prerequisite conditions for checks 3 and 4. Now, the four-step manual test we started with corresponds to these four atomic checks:

Check 1.   Step 1
        → Target Verification
Check 2.   DocumentA → Step 2
        → Target Verification
Check 3.   DocumentB → Step 2
        → Step 3 → Target Verification
Check 4.   DocumentB → Step 2
        → Step 4 → Target Verification

These four checks are independent of each other at check run time, and they are as short as they can be while still verifying the target criteria. They are therefore ready for

implementation according to Atomic Check pattern.

This example can be adapted and/or extended for any SUT that can serialize, persist, and restore state with little quality risk. Even if the end-user experience of the SUT does not include such persistence, if the state can be persisted in a simple and robust serialization mapping, this would allow the checks to be simpler and faster.

Example: creating an atomic check with non-persisted state

Consider an HTTP REST service. After login with successful authentication, the service exports services Alpha and Omega. The business requirements might look like this:

1. Authorization for services needs authentication
    a. Service Alpha (… more detail for Service Alpha)
    b. Service Omega (… more detail for Service Omega)

A manual test might look like:

Step 1. Login, and verify success;

Step 2. Use service Alpha, and verify success;

Step 3. Use service Omega and verify success.

Unfortunately, there is no way of persisting Step 1. The check still needs to log in to use services Alpha and Omega. Since the login is a required step for either of services Alpha and Omega, there is no possibility to remove the login step from the testing of the services. However, we can make a separate check with login success as the verification target. For the Atomic Check pattern, the three checks look like this:

Check 1. Login → verify success.
Check 2. Login → Use service Alpha
      →   verify success.
Check 3. Login → Use service Omega
      → verify success.

If services Alpha and Omega worked the same for an anonymous user, and they did not need authentication, then having just the three checks would not be enough because a login failure might unnecessarily block the automated verification of services Alpha or Omega. A login failure would get less priority from the team in that case because it would be less important for the product. In that case, the Atomic Check pattern calls for six checks rather than three; faster and more scalable checks that do not risk blocking verification of the services on login failure would look like this:

Check 1. Login as anonymous → verify success
Check 2. Login as anonymous → Use service Alpha → verify success
Check 3. Login as anonymous → Use service Omega → verify success
Check 4. Login as verified user → verify success
Check 5. Login as verified user → Use service Alpha → verify success

Check 6. Login as verified user → Use service Omega → verify success

Example: creating an atomic check that spans machines or processes

Suppose the SUT is a computer wrist device or watch, which communicates via Bluetooth™ with a phone or other mobile device. The SUT comes with an app on the phone that is configured to communicate notifications to the device.

The business requirements for this behavior might look like this:

1. Notifications have a status property to reflect whether the wearer has acknowledged the notification.
   a. If the notification is acknowledged on the Bluetooth™ device, the acknowledged status is updated on the Bluetooth™ and the mobile device.

Describe the basic element — what I call an atom — of behavior to verify like this:

1. Given a mobile device and a Bluetooth-connected mobile device, configured to communicate with each other,
2. When a new notification is received on your phone/mobile device, and this notification is communicated to your wrist/Bluetooth device,
3. When the notification is dismissed on the wrist/Bluetooth device,

4. Then the "new notification" flag is cleared on the phone/mobile device.

The target verification of the atomic check is that the dismissal flag is correctly reflected on the mobile device.

Setup steps to configure the two devices are either done in line with the check steps or, for better check run performance, handled by a Precondition Pool pattern implementation.[108] Remaining steps can be done on the devices themselves or software emulations. No modification is needed of the product code itself, but each process must run a simple service and a client to drive and measure the device.

For working code that supports a multi-tier check, see the distributed Sample 3 on pages 173-176.

Steps for two tiers: the phone or mobile device, and the watch or wrist device

1. (on phone) Send notification from phone
2. (on watch) Find verification on watch
3. (on watch) Dismiss verification on watch
4. (on phone) Verify that the "new notification" flag is cleared on the notification

Creating atomic checks from overlapping functional requirements

Figure 28 below is a use case diagram showing a set of five functional requirements for a credit union web portal, ordered by priority from the end-user perspective (i.e. as seen by the credit union customer on the left).

---

[108] See the Precondition Pool pattern on pages 129-134.

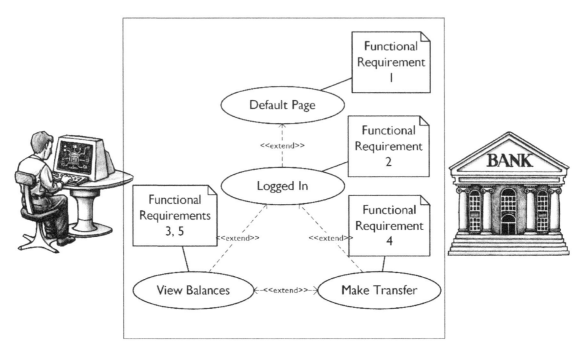

Fig. 28. Use case diagram with overlapping system requirements.

1. The default web page is available.
2. The customer can log in.
3. The customer can view and/or confirm balance(s) on the site.
4. The customer can make a transfer between two of the customer's accounts.
5. The customer can view balances after the transfer to verify correctness in monetary values and/or the customer's intent in doing the transfer.

For best quality information on the portal, one would create four atomic checks for this functionality, ordered here by priority from the business requirements and with the check steps and target verifications listed:

1. Default web page
   a. Request default page
   b. (target verification) page is loaded with core components
2. Customer can log in
   a. Request default page
   b. Enter login data and submit
   c. (target verification) user is authenticated and the correct page is present with core components
3. View/confirm balances
   a. Request default page
   b. Enter login data and submit
   c. Go to balances page
   d. Verify that core elements are present showing balances

e. (target verification) verify all balances

4. Make transfer

  a. Request default page
  b. Enter login data and submit
  c. Select transfer page or operation
  d. Do transfer
  e. View balances
  f. (target verification) verify that all balances are correct

The 4th check given here verifies functional requirements 4 and 5 listed above, which is why there are 4 checks, not 5. It does not add much value to verify the ability to make a transfer without the ability to verify that the result of the transfer is correct. The target verification in this case is verification of expected balances, rather than the transfer step itself, because at the level this app is verified, the transfer cannot be verified to have happened at all without checking the balances.

Theoretically, approaching the condition of infinite low-cost computing resources, the team gets the best value by running all four checks. The extra overhead of running the shorter checks is negligible, but the value in communicating quality is real: if Check 1 fails (the default page is not available) it is a serious, actionable problem and it gets the priority it deserves.

If any of the functional requirements 2, 3, 4, or 5 have questionable reliability or stability, or might undergo a design change in the past or recent future, then there is

significant value to running all four checks. For example, if there is a design change or failure in check 3, the quality of the default page is still being measured independently, which simplifies analysis and transparency. All the data of the check steps is present in the artifact, but it is simpler and more obvious, when there is a separate check for the default page, where the quality issues occur and where they do not.

If the system is both stable and reliable, and there is a need to reduce overhead in the checks, then it is time to consider disabling Check 1 and/or Check 2. Otherwise, and by default, implement and run all the checks.

Review Questions

The answers are on page 210.

1) What is the most basic requirement of the Atomic Check pattern that makes the others possible?
2) What part of the "atomic" aspect is a requirement, and what part is an ideal, rather than an absolute requirement?
3) Why would the common Setup or Teardown pattern interfere with the value of the check run artifacts?
4) Name two advantages to itemizing the business requirements for your software project separately from the testable functional requirements.

Chapter 12
MetaAutomation Pattern: Event-Driven Check

Summary

This pattern is useful when measured behaviors of the SUT respond to events that are either external or otherwise outside of the team's control.

This pattern enables quality automation for decoupled systems joined only by event emitters and consumers.

This pattern might seem to conflict with Paradigm Shift Three (pages 59-66) because the pattern might require faking some dependencies. However, the deferred quality risk is small since the events are so much simpler than external services, in thread timing and in data exchanged as well. This pattern makes that small concession to enable automation to monitor SUT functional quality and performance.

Fig. 29. The system handling and triggering events for Event-Driven Check.

Context

The SUT responds to external events, but functional quality measurements must happen in a repeatable and reliable way to support fast quality measurement, part of ensuring that quality always moves forward.

The Hierarchical Steps[109] and Atomic Check[110] patterns ensure good data and checks that are as simple as possible for the target verification(s).

Problem

Fast and reliable quality measurements need repeatable checks. Repeatable checks depend on deterministic aspects of the SUT.

If uncontrollable loosely coupled external events drive part or all the SUT, conventional means of driving the SUT are not enough for deterministic measurements of functional quality.[111]

Forces

- Some events are external and beyond the team's control, yet important to product behavior.
- Quality measurements of the SUT that avoid introducing quality risks need to measure the complete system, including dependencies.
- Events subscribed to are much simpler than product dependencies on an external service.

Solution

Design checks as with Atomic Check:

- Simple as possible

- Each check runs independently of every other check
- Each check targets one functional requirement
- The hierarchy of check steps document themselves at runtime

However, to drive the SUT, subscribe the product to events generated by the check (or, another part of the quality automation) rather than the external events that are outside ownership of the team.

Drive the events as part of the check.

Measure SUT behavior directly if possible, but if not, subscribe to the correct events and block on them if needed.

Resulting Context

Aspect(s) of SUT behavior that were unavailable to deterministic measurement, are made available.

This solution comes with a small burden to the team: the limited quality risk of subscribing to faked events, and possibly with faked data, must be addressed as soon as is reasonable with other forms of testing the SUT that include all dependencies.

Examples

Example: GUI interface

Event-Driven Check pattern appears in GUI-driven checks, where events to and

---

[109] See the Hierarchical Steps pattern on pages 85-98.

[110] See the Atomic Check pattern on pages 99-119.

[111] This would include threads and events in a GUI that drives part of the SUT, but a GUI is most

often tightly bound to the rest of the SUT. Those threads and events therefore appear internal, so do not need this pattern.

from the GUI interact with common automation tools.

Example: BankingAds

For the running example BankingAds, suppose the app checks for ads based on events from the ad supplier service; the app might change ads during a given banking session, so it needs to get ads based on updates in the results to the ad selection algorithm and the (anonymized) user behavior. Polling is too inefficient and slow, so the app subscribes for events instead.

In the context of an app that is run by automation, if the app subscribes to events not from the ad supplier, but from part of the quality automation infrastructure, the automation can control when ad loads are initiated. This means that, within a bound time span since the ad load is initiated, a new ad is expected to be loaded, and the app can verify the expected ad.

Review Questions

The answers are on page 210.

1) Relative to Atomic Check, is there an added step in automating the SUT as part of Event-Driven Check?
2) Why should the team consider taking on the risk of changing a dependency of the SUT?

Chapter 13
MetaAutomation Pattern: Extension Check

Summary

Suppose the team needs quick, reliable verification of an important quality attribute of the SUT, but the quality to verify is variable, adjustable, or lower priority, e.g., a performance threshold, or there is no way to drive the feature deterministically. An Extension Check avoids these issues by running on data provided with an earlier check result. The downside is that Smart Retry cannot be applied to extension checks; transient or one-off failures would not be visible as such to the team except through the Queryable Quality pattern.

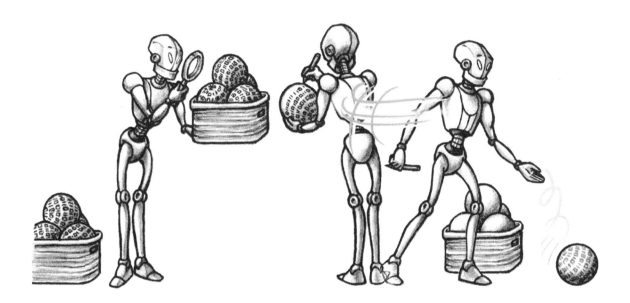

Fig. 30. Automated checks on artifacts of earlier checks for Extension Check.

Context

Hierarchical Steps[112] and Atomic Check[113] deliver very detailed, structured, and trustworthy data on the SUT.

There are systems where automation cannot deterministically drive all behavior aspects. Applying the pattern Event-Driven check might address some of those aspects, but not all.

During a check run, the SUT, instrumented as needed, might show important but non-drivable behaviors or behaviors that are variable in (at least partially) non-deterministic ways. For example, for performance measurement, each step in each check that passed or failed shows milliseconds to completion.

Problem

The team needs to measure some behavioral aspect of the SUT quickly and reliably, but due to non-deterministic timing or variability of the quality aspect, the team does not want to fail atomic checks based on those aspects or run separate checks just for those aspects.

Forces

- There are important non-deterministic behavior aspects of the SUT.
- Repetitive manual tests are boring, unreliable, and expensive.
- Implementing this pattern involves some cost.

- The measurement and reporting on the quality aspect concerned must not interfere with higher-priority checks.
- Performance is a very important aspect of the system.

Solution

Add code to other checks, as needed, to measure and add data in child nodes to enable the extension checks. Do not fail, slow, or block those checks on the extra measurements. Extension checks can measure the non-deterministic quality criteria by reading the artifacts of those earlier check runs that include the software unit(s) where those quality criteria are at issue. The extension checks fail on criteria of the data alone, and only if the sought data is available in the artifacts of the earlier checks.

Resulting Context

The quality automation system can verify non-deterministic or variable aspects of the SUT with fast, scalable checks.

Examples

Example: performance criteria

Performance checks may assert that certain performance criteria are met, and the criteria might be variable over time or dependent on earlier check runs. In those cases, the Extension Check pattern is the ideal way to verify that the SUT meets (potentially complex) performance criteria, because a fail in a performance criterion

---

[112] See the Hierarchical Steps pattern on pages 85-98.

[113] See the Atomic Check pattern on pages 99-119.

will never block other quality measurements.

Example: experiments we cannot control

There are many examples of human endeavors that involve analysis after-the-fact of data from uncontrollable experiments, for example:

- People do significant sociology research, e.g., anthropology studies, without controlled experiments because people are difficult to control, especially because some types of control would be unethical.
- Most Astronomy research uses data from "experiments" in the remote universe that humans do not have the power to start or control.

Example: BankingAds

For the BankingAds app, although the ads come from an external company, people on the project still must verify that the ads are served correctly in response to end-user activities, balances, etc. and of course asynchronously during other activities. The new-ad event gets a hook that adds information about the ad to the check as the check is running, so the timing, identity, type etc. of the ad shows up in the artifact of the check.

After the SUT-driving check run, an Extension Check does the analysis to decide if the ads are correct or not, with acceptable timing and other criteria.

Review Questions

The answers are on pages 210-211.

1) Why might the team not consider the Extension Check pattern to gate check-ins of SUT code to a shared repository?
2) Describe a risk of using performance checks to gate check-ins.

Chapter 14
MetaAutomation Pattern: Precondition Pool

Summary

If systems give prepared resources independently of the check itself, the check can be simpler, faster, and more reliable. Such a check will create more focused quality knowledge, and faster.

Precondition Pool is about managing preconditions for the check runs that can be handled asynchronously and out-of-process for the checks that need them.

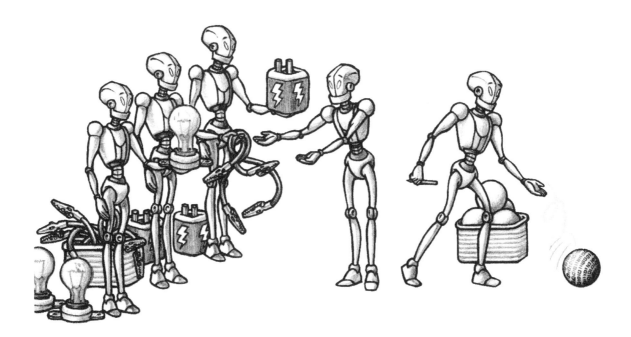

Fig. 31. Three Precondition Pool instances at left.

Context

Checks focus on target verifications. Verifications need resources that may be runtime-independent of the target.

For example, every check runs in an environment. The environment is a precondition of the check run.

Depending on the SUT, quality automation can break out other resources as well. For example, user accounts, documents, database images, externally-facing accounts, may all be part of a check but runtime-independent of the target verification or verifications.

Problem

If every check runs with all preconditions created in-line with the check, the run will be relatively slow and complex. It will have more potential points of failure than needed for a given quality measurement. Over many check runs, more potential points of failure will cause more blocked quality measurements and more complex checks. These problems reduce the speed, reliability, and value of the quality knowledge.

Forces

- Checks use resources such as environments, test user accounts, documents, and other objects with specific states.
- To the extent that the quality automation system queues up preconditions before the check run starts, the checks run faster.
- Simpler checks will always run more reliably.
- Simpler checks deliver more focused SUT knowledge.
- Moving preconditions out-of-line and out-of-process from the check can add implementation complexity and development overhead to the overall quality automation solution.

Solution

For your SUT, consider which resources a pool can manage out-of-process to the check itself. You may already be managing automation environments, with automated choice of environments; if so, you are using the Precondition Pool pattern already.

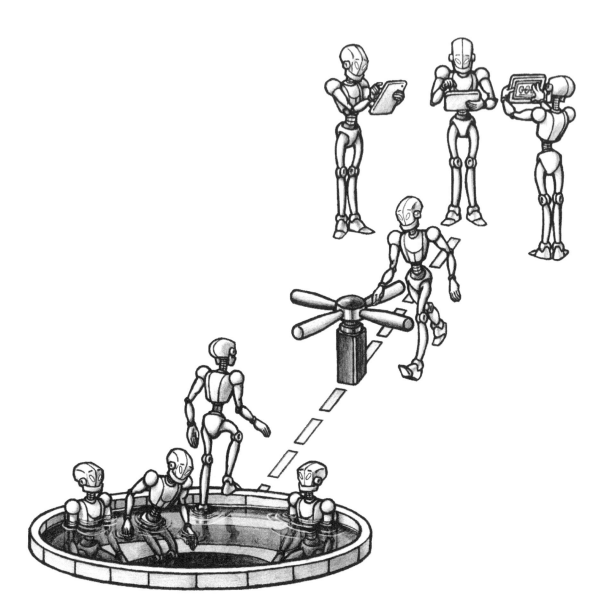

Fig. 32. Precondition Pool resource flow.

For each resource type, manage it as an independent pool, completely out-of-process relative to the check run or runs. Quality automation checks out pool items as needed for use with a check, then checks them back in. The pool implementation restores them as necessary to the desired state. The pool keeps enough such items that they enable the check run to run at optimal speed. Even if the check run uses so many pooled resources that the pool takes significant maintenance overhead during the run, there is little added overhead compared to the case where the resources are not pooled. The pool can also expand to handle more such resources and keep them at the ready, so when a check run is launched, it completes sooner. The checks themselves are more reliable and simpler, so create better and more useful data on the SUT. The entire check run scales better with resources, too.

Precondition Pool instances can also exist for sub-types of resources. For example, there can be a Precondition Pool instance for each role of a test user, for an application that uses role-based security.

Resulting Context

By helping the checks run quicker and with more focused quality data, Precondition Pool helps the Parallel Run[114] and Smart Retry[115] patterns run more effectively, and it reduces the duration of the set of checks for a given run.

If a given Precondition Pool takes significant computing resources, then it might be desirable to cache many instances of those resources up front so that when a check run begins, those resources are available to expedite the checks and deliver results faster.

With the preconditions handled separately, the checks are simpler and the data that results from running the checks is therefore easier and more valuable to work with.

With the pools handling errors associated with managing the preconditions, the checks have fewer points of potential failure and so are more reliable.

Examples

Example: thread pool

Operating systems and services use thread pools to enable more efficient management of the threads needed. These are analogous to Precondition Pool instances, and the advantages are similar.

Example: precursor pattern

The Setup and Teardown phases of the Four-Phase Test pattern named by Meszaros are precursors to Precondition Pool because the intent of setup and teardown is of a "fixture," i.e., something that needs to happen to support the test, but which is not the target of the test (Meszaros 2007). That so many people used the pattern is therefore an example of managing check resources as preconditions. With Four-Phase Test, however, the phases always happen in-line, which has negative consequences on check complexity, reliability, performance, scale, and the quality of the artifact data.

Examples: familiar check resources

The Precondition Pool pattern applies where checks run across different machines or virtual machines. In the lab or cloud where the SUT is configured and running (or, the client part of it), a pool implementation manages the available environments where the SUT runs.

---

[114] See the Parallel Run pattern on pages 135-140.

[115] See the Smart Retry pattern on pages 141-150.

Other examples of external resources that can be managed with this solution include:

- user accounts of diverse types and states
- internal or external databases of test data or standard product configurations
- documents of certain states or storage locations

etc.

Discovering and characterizing the pattern creates opportunities for the team. If the system uses more Precondition Pool instances to manage more resources, the checks will be more scalable, faster, simpler, and more effective.

Example: BankingAds

For the BankingAds app example, Precondition Pool applies to managing the many environments in which the checks can run scalably, as well as customer accounts of diverse types and balances. Having pools to handle user accounts makes the checks simpler, faster, and more scalable, and thereby shortens the overall check run and improves the quality of data from the check run.

Review Questions

The answers are on page 211.

1) Describe how an implementation of Precondition Pool is an improvement over the common Setup and Teardown patterns.
2) Name two advantages to adding one or more implementations of Precondition Pool to the quality automation of your software product.

Chapter 15
MetaAutomation Pattern: Parallel Run

Summary
If checks run in parallel, they scale with available computing resources. Using more computing resources shortens the time a developer or team must wait for the complete run of the check set.

Context
The Atomic Check[116] and Precondition Pool[117] patterns ensure that checks are optimally fast and run independently of each other.

Precondition Pool supplies preconditions for the checks to run, speeding and simplifying the checks.

Computing resources are increasingly available at decreasing costs.

Problem
If checks run sequentially, for a large set of checks, the entire check run can take a long time.

The business needs to run many checks quickly.

---

[116] See the Atomic Check pattern on pages 99-119.

[117] See the Precondition Pool pattern on pages 129-134.

Fig. 33. Three instances of running automation for Parallel Run.

Forces

- The team needs a set of checks to run as fast as possible.
- The number of checks to run might be very large.
- There is some development cost to implement Parallel Run.
- There is some runtime cost and network overhead to interface with it, to enable the checks to run in parallel.
- Computing resources are becoming increasingly available and inexpensive.

Solution

With a Precondition Pool implementation handling many machines and environments, run the checks in parallel (Caspar et al. 2014) (Garg and Datta 2013).

Without parallelization, the checks all must run sequentially, as the UML sequence diagram Figure 34 shows:

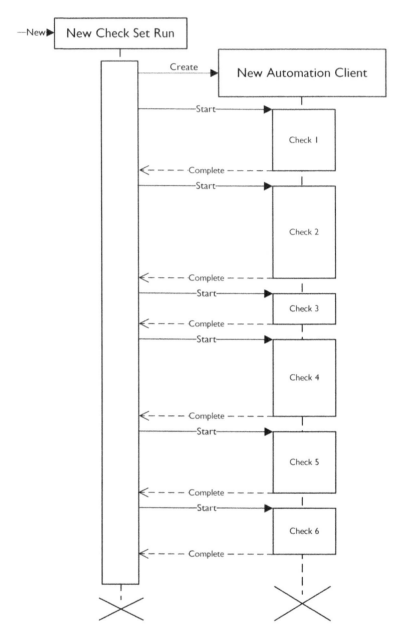

Fig. 34. Sequence diagram of checks running sequentially.

With parallelization, the checks can run on an arbitrary number of clients, so they run faster. Given many clients, the speed at which the checks run is almost arbitrarily fast. Figure 35 shows the speed increase with the same checks run across three clients:

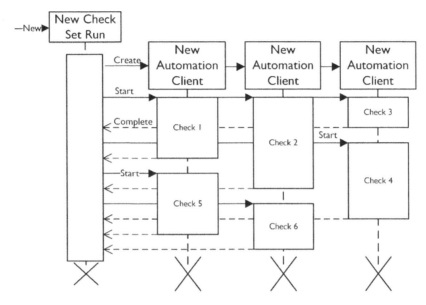

Fig. 35. Checks running in parallel.

Resulting Context

Since they can scale with computing resources, the checks can run faster overall, and potentially much faster, making it possible to run a much larger number of checks and get much more data on the SUT.

Smart Retry[118] is now effective because a retry of a given check will happen quickly with minimal impact on the overall check run.

Queryable Quality[119] is more effective because there is more data on the product.

Examples

Example: parallel processing

This pattern appears in, e.g., web servers for high-volume sites that handle requests on different threads, cores, processors, and/or machines. Weather simulations also depend on massively parallel processing.

Example: BankingAds

For the BankingAds example, the number of checks is quite large, and the app is

---

[118] See the Smart Retry pattern on pages 141-150.

[119] See the Queryable Quality pattern on pages 155-158.

crucial to people, which makes functional quality very important. The Atomic Check pattern enables each check to run independently, so there is an opportunity as well as an incentive to run the checks in parallel across an arbitrarily large number of virtual machines. The check run can therefore be very fast and integrate into the development process with manageable disruption.

Review Questions

The answers are on page 211.

1) What aspect of Atomic Check makes Parallel Run possible?
2) Name a capability that Parallel Run offers, to help DevOps.

Chapter 16
MetaAutomation Pattern: Smart Retry

Summary

It is a common pattern to retry a check on fail. But without much data on what the check is doing or where it failed, only a "dumb" retry is possible. Root cause of a failure, or whether a check reproduces a failure, is unknown to the automation. There is opportunity cost of not having the data: the clarity needed to act (or, decide whether an action is needed) is only possible through manual follow-up (Jiang et al. 2017).

With detailed and trustworthy runtime data on how automation drives the SUT, quality automation can include knowledge of root cause and failure persistence in automated decisions. This delivers more value for the team, and more quickly.

Context

The Hierarchical Steps[120] pattern gives detailed and highly trustworthy data on SUT behavior, including showing root cause of a given check failure.

---

[120] See the Hierarchical Steps pattern on pages 85-98.

Fig. 36. Automation choosing checks for Smart Retry.

The Atomic Check[121] pattern ensures that the check is as simple as possible, given the target, so the data is focused.

The Atomic Check and Parallel Run[122] patterns make it possible to run many checks and retry any failed check quickly.

Sometimes the checks fail.

Check failures might be easily reproducible, or not.

Problem

With conventional practices, on a team that uses automation for quality, false positives may be a significant business cost as well as an annoyance. They tend to block informative quality measurements and decrease trust in check results, therefore interfering with the value of the quality automation.

The team benefits from reproducing some check failures through clarity, more quality knowledge, or just the trust that it is not a one-off failure. If the check cannot be reproduced, that is valuable information too; but with conventional approaches none of that data is available to or from quality automation.

Forces

- A check that fails due to an external resource, but would likely succeed on retry, might be a false positive and not actionable by the team.

- Interrupting team members with false positives is a significant cost to the business.
- If the quality automation system can reproduce a given failure before presenting it to the business, that increases trust in and actionability of the failure.
- A failure that cannot be reproduced is not necessarily a false positive; depending on root cause, it might be a sign of a bug in the SUT.
- In some systems, e.g., avionics, any failure may be significant.
- Implementation costs for this pattern include configuration for what criteria to use to compare failures and to determine which failures lead to retry.

Solution

The data in each failed check shows the root cause with detail on driving the SUT. Configure the quality automation system to either run the check again in every case of failure or run it again only if the root cause is not in the SUT — for example, in an external dependency which timed out — or otherwise not actionable by the dev team.

Figure 37 below shows a simple implementation of Smart Retry that assumes that all check failures are candidates for retries, no matter the root cause of the check failure:

---

[121] See the Atomic Check pattern on pages 99-119.

[122] See the Parallel Run pattern on pages 135-140.

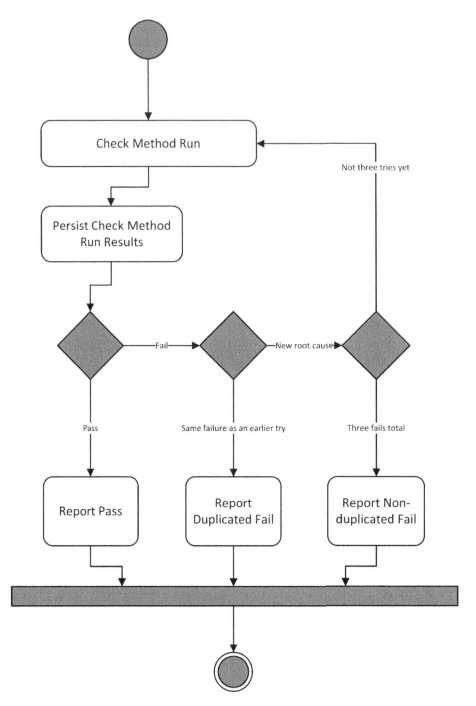

Fig. 37. The Smart Retry activity for the case where all failed checks are retry candidates.

A slightly more complex implementation does not always retry. For some failure cases in some SUTs, retry is not desired because the failure is always important and actionable. The detailed artifact from a failed check has the data to decide whether this is the case. For example, a non-deterministic failure due to SUT code might be actionable, and not a candidate for retry.

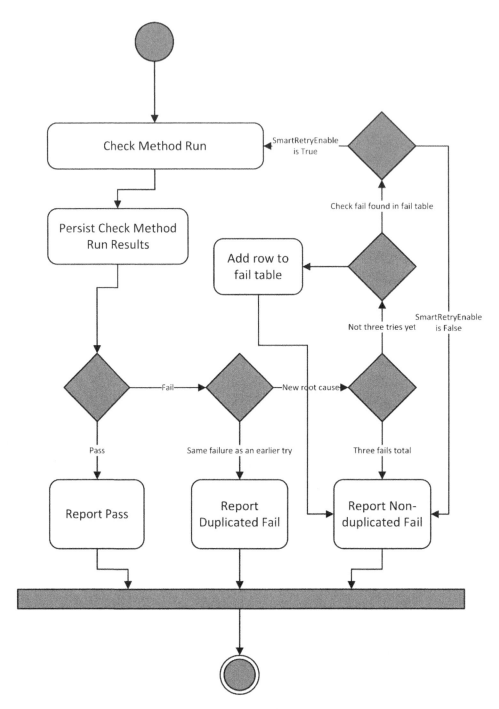

Fig. 38. The Smart Retry activity for the case where no retry is the default.

Figure 38 shows the case where, given certain failures, no retry happens. A table

of root cause information with the manually enabled SmartRetryEnable flag enabling retry, decides whether there is a retry. This could also work with a quick data-driven set of logic tests.

Smart Retry bundles the information from retried checks before the data is available to the rest of the quality automation system. Here are four potential cases, and how Smart Retry might handle them:

1. For checks that failed, but the immediate retry passed, Smart Retry bundles data from both check attempts and marks the bundle as a pass.

2. For checks that failed, when the immediate retry reproduced the error, automation bundles data from both check attempts as a fail. Since the failure reproduced automatically, it has improved value and is more actionable for the business than if it were just an isolated failure.

3. For checks that fail and map to a retry, but then fails again in a way that does not map to a retry, the resulting bundle is a failure with the non-retry check fail given higher priority because it is an action item for a developer.

4. For checks that fail, and then fail again with different root cause that also maps to enable a retry, and the third try fails to reproduce either of the first two failures, data from all three check attempts is bundled and

shown as a non-reproduced fail. If one of the failures does not map to enable a retry, it is more likely immediately actionable, so it can be marked or ordered at higher priority for the rest of the quality automation system.

The three working sample solutions show data-driven timeout configuration: The timeout in milliseconds for a given step is defined, and can be changed, in the XML node for that step in the artifact from the previous run. This is useful for configuring timeout for optimal check run duration in case of failure-prone checks.

Configuring timeout for failure-prone checks

Sometimes checks that depend on services tend to time out. A potential solution is to increase the time-out time so that the check simply hangs for a longer time, until either the service responds or the request times out. The team might consider the question: Will Smart Retry really help in this case? Is it more effective to simply increase the timeout for the operation?

Increasing the timeout too much (e.g., to 300,000 milliseconds or 5 minutes for a web request) will cause the check run to take longer in those cases where the service simply fails to respond, for example, due to a bug on the service side, server restart, rebalancing, etc. Timing out, failing the check, and re-running it through the Smart Retry implementation will likely be faster,[123] and if the server failure-to-respond issue persists, that will still likely take less time to reproduce that failure with a reasonable timeout (e.g., 5 seconds) than it will to run the check once and time out at something like 5 minutes. In addition, with Smart Retry pattern implementation, the artifact data is more conclusive and actionable: the check with retry(s) has reproduced the timeout, and the fact is reported along with all the artifact data.

With traditional automation, for checks that are prone to one-off failures, the team must make a choice between two costs: either the authors do added work up front to make the flaky checks more robust, e.g., by adding sleeps and/or seeking out other triggering events, or the team suffers the cost of checks which fail intermittently. Another common pattern is to designate some checks as flaky and just run them 3 times every time and discard the failures.

Smart Retry makes this choice unnecessary and avoids both the up-front cost and the deferred one. Checks do not have to be extremely reliable, just reliable enough that they do not often fail for the same non-actionable reason twice in a row on a retry. The team is not affected by one-off failures, although the artifacts from these failures are saved just the same for later analysis if that is desired.

With no need for three tries for every flaky check, and no need for excessive timeouts, Smart Retry reduces the time for the check run to complete.

Resulting Context

The Automated Triage[124] implementation will not receive false positives, so the team will not get any such unnecessary distractions. See above in the solution for this pattern (section 2.7.5) which failures are actionable, and therefore worthy of a targeted notification.

A quality portal implemented with Queryable Quality[125] shows all check results, including checks that passed the first time and checks that experienced failures. For retried checks, the portal displays the resulting bundle of check tries the same way as a non-retried check is, with a pass or fail status depending on the status of the bundle. Drill-down exposes the multiple tries of the check.

Examples

Example: "Retry" pattern

Microsoft, Google, and others use a pattern called "Retry" which is to simply retry a check on failure, up to three tries total. This is useful for automation on, e.g., a graphical user interface (GUI) or web browser and where the synchronization points are inaccessible, not available at all,

---

[123] This depends on the complexity of the service that is prone to time out in this context. The more complex the service, the more likely that there are underlying issues that will not be resolved with a long timeout, and therefore it is likely that a retry after a relatively short timeout will be faster for the overall check run.

[124] See the Automated Triage pattern on pages 151-154.

[125] See the Queryable Quality pattern on pages 155-158.

for some reason too difficult or expensive to access, or they time out sometimes anyway. This is a much simpler version of the pattern presented here.

However, applying the simpler retry pattern is risky: it makes no attempt to distinguish between failures due to unavoidable race conditions in a GUI or actionable (and, potentially fixable) race conditions in the SUT. A retry that passes could temporarily hide an actionable failure, and as a result, the bug might never be discovered because (in the absence of the Hierarchical Steps pattern) the data is not persisted.

In the Office team at Microsoft, the complexity of the SUT is such that it includes nondeterministic business logic conditions (see the Extension Check pattern on pages 125-128). The team uses the Retry pattern here (Roseberry 2017).

Unlike the Smart Retry pattern, however, the Retry pattern has no capability for deciding at check run time whether a specific failure cause is reproduced or whether, based on root cause of failure, the retry should happen in the first place.

Microsoft also documents a "Retry pattern" for product code (MSDN 2015).

Example: BankingAds

Given that the end-user interface for the app is a web browser, there may be automation failures due to race conditions in the client interface. These are candidates for retry according to Smart Retry. If the check reproduces the timeout failure at the same leaf step, then the failure becomes actionable by either someone in the QA role (who might increase a timeout, depending on other timing information for the check) or a developer who works with the interface.

For checks that discover an incorrect monetary balance, no retry is in order; that failure is actionable.

Example: web site with AJAX

Suppose the SUT is a web site, with multiple services providing data and interactivity.[126] Business logic on the web server is fairly complex. The team doing quality infrastructure for the SUT decides to apply the Smart Retry pattern for the configurable case; as described above, a smart retry does not happen by default per this design.

With many checks run against the site, the results (and the artifacts) show several intermittent check failures for which root cause is not clear. The AJAX request that would refresh the page simply fails with an HTTP 500 error.

A client with hooks to the JavaScript in the browser drives the automation, but the failure is intermittent and there is no clear way to reproduce it. Before the team identifies this issue as an external one, more information is needed to find root cause. The automation authors can help here by supplementing the artifact information with data – one or more

---

[126] Thanks to Alan Page for inspiring this example.

name/value pairs, where the value comes from server-side logs related to the issue – in the preliminary steps.[127]

With more information from the web server in the artifacts for the checks – for the few checks that fail with the intermittent issue as described above – the failures are brought to the attention of a developer who works with the web site's dependencies. The developer finds root cause for some of these cases. It turns out to be a product bug, so she enters the bug and fixes the issue or sends the (now nicely detailed, with an automated reproduction) bug to the developer owner.

With the benefit of the Automated Triage pattern, the developer can also link the bug to one or more of the check run results (i.e., the artifacts) that show this failure. The Automated Triage pattern and the Quality Portal concept enable the automated correlation of future check failures with this or many such failures by the notification engine, and hence the bug that the developer owned above will become part of the regression testing in product quality.

Review Questions

The answers are on pages 211-212.

1) Name two advantages of an implementation of Smart Retry vs. the traditional Retry pattern.
2) What pattern(s) makes Smart Retry possible?

---

[127] See "Preliminary steps" on page 103.

Chapter 17
MetaAutomation Pattern: Automated Triage

Summary

Given that checks have detailed, trustworthy data on the SUT, and failed checks know about root cause of failure, Automated Triage shows how to automatically send targeted notifications as needed.

Context

Hierarchical Steps[128] gives very detailed, structured, and trustworthy data on every check run, including cause of failure at all hierarchy levels for those checks that fail.

---

[128] See the Hierarchical Steps pattern on pages 85-98.

Fig. 39. Automation directs notifications based on check results.

Atomic Check[129] gives checks that are as simple as possible, given the target verification or verification cluster. The detailed data in the targeted check shows who gets the notification.

Smart Retry[130] can show whether a given check failure is a false positive or, in case of retry, whether automation can reproduce the failure with the same root cause.

Problem

With conventional "test automation," all check failures trigger notifications, or are part of notifications, sent to many people on the team. It then becomes a manual task to decide who, if anyone, is the best person to take an action item based on a given check failure. This is an unnecessary distraction and cost to the business.

The recipients of such notifications are less likely to act on them promptly if they know that the probability of them being a significant and actionable email is low.

The business needs targeted push notifications, but how to send them only to those who need to know?

Forces

- There are business costs when team members receive notifications that are not actionable; the team gets distracted, it decreases trust in the quality automation system, and as a result, decreases attention to the important quality-related notifications.
- There is overhead to implementing and configuring the Automated Triage pattern.
- There is cost and risk in the QA role to *manually* triage and forward certain check results to the right people.

Solution

Implement a rules engine, configured with criteria to choose based on data stored in the check failure. The rules engine would find root cause of the failure based on check result data, e.g.

- What was the failed check step, or the path to the step?
- What was the exception thrown?

and figure out what developer(s) is/are responsible, if any.

This rules engine would forward check failures with notification(s) only to targeted people or a small discussion list.

By default, the notification would go to QA role only, or a specific person within that role. A check fail always sends at least one notification.

Notifications sent might include basic data on the failure, including

---

[129] See the Atomic Check pattern on pages 99-119.

[130] See the Smart Retry pattern on pages 141-150.

- whether the quality automation system has reproduced the failure
- whether this failure exists and is correlated with a known bug
- a link to a Queryable Quality implementation view of the failure[131]

etc.

Resulting Context

The notifications go to those who would act on them, or to a discussion list in case there is a small set of people, one of whom must act on it.

The notifications may also include links to an implementation of Queryable Quality, so recipients can investigate further.

Receiving only targeted messages from the quality automation system means there are many fewer of them in recipients' inboxes, and these messages are far more likely to get the right priority. This is important to keep SUT behavioral quality always moving forward.

Examples

Example: Office

A simpler and more modest system for directing notifications is in use in the Office team at Microsoft (Roseberry 2017). The available artifact data is much more modest than what MetaAutomation enables, so options for directing the notifications are correspondingly simpler.

Example: BankingAds

For the BankingAds app, Automated Triage directs actionable communications to specific people or groups. For example, if a web page object timeout was reproduced by the Smart Retry pattern, a notification goes to a person or list in the QA role. In case of an incorrect bank balance, a correctly configured Smart Retry implementation would not do a retry, and a notification would go directly to an owning developer or select group of them.

Review Questions

The answers are on page 212.

1) How does Automated Triage help software development go faster?
2) Why is Automated Triage so important to clarity and transparency around the team?

---

[131] See the Queryable Quality pattern on pages 155-158.

Chapter 18
MetaAutomation Pattern: Queryable Quality

Summary

Queryable Quality provides rich access to quality data on the SUT, for anyone on the team concerned with quality, including QA, test, the dev team, etc. Team members can, if they wish, drill down from a brief description of the check, to the business-facing steps, all the way to the technology-facing steps and measurements on the SUT.[132] All the check result data is available for robust query and analysis as well.

Context

The Hierarchical Steps[133] pattern, Atomic Check,[134] Precondition Pool,[135] and Parallel Run[136] give vast amounts of highly structured and trustworthy data on product quality.

---

[132] To see this in action, run any of the samples and view the results in an XML-supporting browser. The samples are on pages 161-176.

[133] See the Hierarchical Steps pattern on pages 85-98.

[134] Atomic Check pattern on pages 99-119.

[135] Precondition Pool pattern on pages 129-134.

[136] Parallel Run pattern on pages 135-140.

Fig. 40. A team member querying check result data.

Smart Retry[137] ensures that non-actionable failures do not interrupt people's work flow.

Automated Triage[138] includes links to Queryable Quality with sent notifications.

Team members will want access to the detailed and trustworthy data on the SUT for performance and functionality. They will want to do query and analysis on that rich quality knowledge.

Problem

The business requires role-appropriate transparency into SUT functional and performance quality, so anyone on the team can access what is going on with the product, in the correct detail level, and in a meaningful way.

Forces

- Quality data must be easily viewable, link-able and queryable by team members.
- The data generated by the quality automation must be persisted and served with read-only access for the lifetime of the SUT.
- Implementing and supporting a Queryable Quality portal (or, quality portal) has cost.

Solution

Implement and deploy an interactive portal, client or other human-computer interface that is internal to the company.

The portal enables rich and configurable query, display, drill-down and export capability.

With drill-down capability, while the business-facing view of a check is at and near the displayed root node of the hierarchy, drill-down is available to show more detail as desired. If they wish, team members can drill all the way to the atomic technology-facing steps and measurements of the SUT. Operations and measurements on the SUT are completely self-documenting, and Queryable Quality surfaces this information to the team for both casual perusal and deep analysis.

Resulting Context

All data on the SUT for behavior and performance is available for viewing and querying by anyone on the team who is concerned with quality. Visibility into product quality is radically better across the team as compared to common practices.

There is transparency across the team into the work of the developers and the QA role.

Queryable Quality surfaces and shares detailed data to augment and help meetings and discussions around the team.

Examples

Example: intranet portals

Intranet portals are a common pattern at companies. Intranet portals into product

---

[137] Smart Retry pattern on pages 141-150.

[138] Automated Triage pattern on pages 151-154.

quality information are a common pattern at software companies.

Example: BankingAds

For the BankingAds app, a quality portal is useful to all team members concerned with quality.

Manual testers look to see what scenarios or features are not covered by the automation, so they will know where to explore the product.

Developers use it when they get a notification about some failure, and they follow the link to the portal to see all the detail of the failure. That is how, for example, it is clear that, given the example of a check failure above, on pages 97-98, the root cause is a read-only field in a web page that needs to be writeable. Developers have little need to reproduce the problem and debug through now, because they probably have enough information already to fix it.

Product owners, leads and managers have a clear view into what part of BankingAds works, how reliably it works, and what part does not work yet. They therefore can see clearly into the productivity of people in the QA and the developer roles.

People in the QA role use it to watch the BankingAds' app health as well as the health of their quality systems.

Accountants doing work for Sarbanes-Oxley (i.e., company valuation, including software assets, and specific to the United States) have access to highly detailed, structured, direct, and highly credible information on the quality of the BankingAds product and quality trends over time.

If the BankingAds project team crosses geographies or cultures, Queryable Quality creates a new level of transparency in quality across the teams and vastly improves communication on quality issues.

With telemetry on the BankingAds app, there is customer usage data that can supplement check results. The team can study correlations between changes in app behavior or performance with the telemetry data, through the Queryable Quality site.

Review Questions

The answers are on page 212.

1) List three types of data that an Atomic Check implementation makes available to Queryable Quality that traditional "test automation" does not.
2) Describe some aspects of Atomic Check that make Queryable Quality more valuable
3) How can a quality portal help with SOX compliance?

Chapter 19
Future Patterns for MetaAutomation

MetaAutomation will have more patterns in future. Just like the ones described here, the future patterns will address quality automation: the problem space between driving the SUT for verifications and measurements of functional correctness and performance, and the business that consumes that information. There will be patterns to address needs not covered by the patterns described in this book.

As Mark Tomlinson told me on a Skype conference

> *The less we hold onto something, the more it can grow. (Tomlinson 2017b)*

To become a living pattern language, MetaAutomation needs community. It needs people to not just educate on, execute and use the patterns, but also to confirm the existing patterns, evolve them or create better expressions of the patterns, and develop new ones.

Evolution and improvement in the existing patterns, and discovery, writing and teaching of new ones, will make MetaAutomation better and increase value to software quality practitioners and their teams.

For example, the Hierarchical Steps pattern could be a valuable tool in improving transparency into results provided by machine learning software.

Fig. 41. Thinking about innovative solutions to add value in the quality automation space.

For the reader who would like to get involved, or has questions on this or related material, please see the LinkedIn Group "Quality Automation."[139]

---

[139] The "Quality Automation" group is here, but you might have to login to LinkedIn before following the URL https://www.linkedin.com/groups/13563800

Section III

Sample Solutions

Chapter 20
How to Use the Samples

Overview

Samples 1, 2 and 3 are hosted on GitHub® and accessible through the site http://MetaAutomation.net. Each of the three samples can be downloaded separately and un-compressed into your workspace. Each has an HTML document that is the installation and simple usage manual, and the sample in the form of a Visual Studio 2017 solution. They were developed using the free "Community 2017" version of Visual Studio. You will need a version of Visual Studio[140] to run the samples as they are presented, although most of the projects are written in platform-independent C#.[141]

Each sample implements Atomic Check and a simple version of Parallel Run, and shows the following capabilities:

1. Recording all interactions with the system
2. Structured artifact of pure data from a run of a check
3. Self-documenting check steps from source code
4. Hierarchical check steps
5. In-line performance information for each step
6. Data-driven configurable timeout for each step
7. Check step results in-line: pass, fail, or blocked
8. Flexible insertion of added structured data from code

The services can be reimplemented on any service platform, because the communication protocols used are all XML-based.

---

[140] The free community 2017 version is here https://www.visualstudio.com/downloads/.

[141] Other than the service components, the samples are implemented in platform-independent C#.

9. Structured stack traces in case of check fail, for exceptions and recursive inner exceptions

10. Debug capabilities to induce check failure at any step or over rolling steps in the check artifact

In addition, Sample 2 demonstrates

1. Running checks in parallel, in different processes on the same machine

2. Individual checks can run across any number of processes on a single machine. This is useful for instrumenting the product or measuring services that can only be accessed from a different process

Sample 3 goes further, to show

1. Running checks in parallel, across different processes and different machines

2. Flexible hierarchical structure for running checks across any number of tiers

3. Flexibility in user identities for running the checks

Sample 1 is much simpler to set up and run, so it is recommended to run and play with Sample 1 before the others. Samples 2 or 3 are the ones you are more likely to extend, customize, or refactor into a solution for your team.

Sample 1 also includes a tutorial. One of the HTML documents in the solution for Sample 1 is for the tutorial.

The Samples page on MetaAutomation.net also links to the Check Step Editor project on GitHub. The project and source code are there for reference, but installation is easier when done directly in Visual Studio with the Extensions menu under Tools.

See the tutorial in Sample 1 for more information on installing and using this extension.

The Cycle of Driving a Check and Persisting Results

The artifact of a check run forms the record of a check run, but it is also needed to drive the next run of the same check. Figure 42 opposite illustrates this.

This works because the artifact is an XML document that has information about running the check, outside the context of the code methods themselves, including:

1. The hierarchy of steps in the check run (assuming it has successfully run to completion at least once);

2. Methods for the different components of the check;

3. Timeouts configured directly in the XML artifact;

4. Custom data;

And, for Sample 3,

1. The user context(s) for the check run;

2. Target machines or tiers on which the different components of the check are executed.

See the instructions that come with the samples for more information.

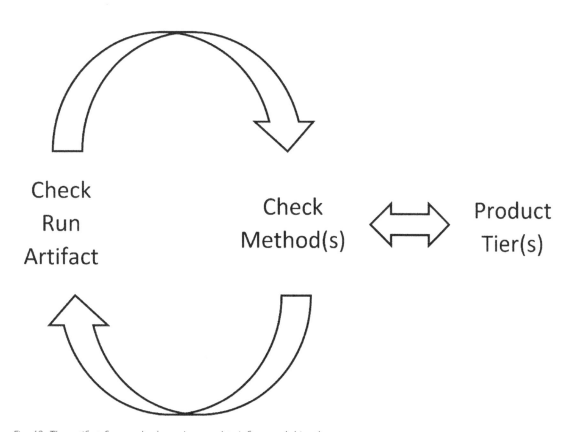

Fig. 42. The artifact from a check run is reused to inform and drive the next run.

The Check Step Editor Visual Studio Extension

This extension simplifies adding or removing check steps in the C# code to work with the libraries of the samples.[142]

For more information on Check Step Editor, see the tutorial that comes with Sample 1.

---

[142] There are such extensions available for Visual Studio 2015 and 2017.

Review Questions

The answers are on page 213.

1) What does it mean that check steps are "self-documenting?"

2) How are the check steps hierarchical?

3) How does a check run "know" what all the steps are, even if they are "blocked?"

Chapter 21
MetaAutomation Sample 1

Overview

See the section "How to Use the Samples" on pages 163-166 and the instructions included with Sample 1 to get it running.

Sample 1 is the simplest sample of the three. It runs the checks in series, all in the same process.

It has three example checks:

1. A very simple check with dummy code to show how the infrastructure works
2. A simple check of a web page that is built to succeed for about 20% of the requests, or fail in one of four different ways, each failure occurring for roughly 20% of requests.
3. A very simple example of how to implement a negative check

What Sample 1 Demonstrates

Self-documenting hierarchical steps

These are in the C# code of the sample, for the six sample checks in MetaAutomation Sample 1.

To find the code for the check, look in the artifact from the last run of the check for the CheckMethodName and/or the CheckMethodGuid, and find them in the CheckMethods project of the solution.

The check code defines the steps and the step hierarchy, and of course what happens in each step. A method call is like a self-documenting step, named after the method name.

The higher-level (i.e., parent) steps define the operations of the step relative to the business-facing description of what the step is doing. The higher-level steps use the same terms as the functional requirements.

The lower-level steps get more granular, and the leaf steps (i.e. the steps with no child steps) define the technology-facing operations of the check. For the most useful detail in the check run artifact, including actionability of a failure and record over time of what happened with the check driving the product, in each leaf step it is ideal to have no more than one code statement that can fail.

Things to Try

Example 1, the simple one-tier check, and brief tutorial

This tutorial will demonstrate

- setting timeouts
- viewing blocked check steps
- inserting custom data into the check artifact

Build (or rebuild) the complete solution.

Run Sample 1 several times. The artifact files are placed in a subdirectory of the solution: "Artifacts\Example_1_SimpleOneTierCheck." Open the artifacts that result from running this check and toggle between them to see how they are the same vs. how they differ.

Open the source code file Example_1_SimpleOneTierCheck.cs in the CheckMethods project. Increase the sleep interval in the step "Step 3" from 55 to 1500 milliseconds. Rebuild the solution and run the check again.

Open the artifact that resulted from that check run (and, be careful to get the actual results; it will be the most recent artifact file created, and the file CheckMap.xml points to it with attribute CurrentCheckRunArtifact). Note that the longer sleep causes the check to fail by timeout due to the breakpoint delay.[143] Look at the CheckStep elements in the artifact that represent the steps of the check and see values for XML attributes msTimeLimit and msTimeElapsed. Find the step(s) that timed out due to the delay. Look in the DataElement children of the CheckFailData element the names "ExceptionType" and "ExceptionMessage;" note that Step 3 timed out and failed the check.

In the CheckStep element with name "Step 3," edit the artifact to increase the msTimeLimit to 2000, i.e., 2 seconds. Save this artifact and run the check again. Open the artifact file just created. Note that this time — according to the exception message — it was step 2 that caused the timeout.

In the latest artifact from the check, increase the msTimeLimit for step 2 from 200 to 1800 milliseconds. Save the artifact file, run the check again and open the artifact that resulted. Look under CheckFailData to see the exception information. This time, it was the overall check that determined the timeout!

---

[143] If the check succeeds at this point, it might be running on an old executable. In that case, rebuild the solution again, or restart Visual Studio and rebuild all, then run it again.

Go back to the C# file Example_1_SimpleOneTierCheck.cs and look at the code for Step 1. Increase the sleep from 50 milliseconds to 1200. Rebuild the solution.

Look at the XML artifact file again and see the CheckStep for Step 1. The msTimeLimit should be 800 milliseconds. This time Step 1 is expected to time out at 800 milliseconds, while sleeping for 1200 milliseconds. Run the check to find out if this works.

The expected behavior is that Step 1 has timed out, and steps 2 and 3 are now marked as "blocked" because they never ran at all. Open the artifact file that resulted and see if this worked.

Go back to the C# file and set both sleeps (Step 1 and Step 3) at 50 milliseconds. Add a line of code after the sleep in Step 3, and type "Check.SetCustomDataCheckStep("Current time", "Lunchtime"). Rebuild the solution and run the check. Load the latest artifact file that this created. See the DataElement with "Current Time" and "Lunchtime" that is a child of Step 3.

The method Check.SetCustomDataCheckStep can insert any kind of instrumentation data from the check code or the SUT.

Example 2, the web page built to fail randomly, and brief tutorial

This section demonstrates how checks with hierarchical steps handle and report check failures.

Edit the check map file CheckMap.xml. Un-comment the XML for the Check element for check Example_2_CheckOfWebPageBuiltToFailRandomly. Optionally, comment out the Check element for check "Example_1_SimpleOneTierCheck" so it does not run each time first.

Run this check — the check on the failing web page —about a dozen times. Note that the longest this check will run is about 15 seconds; the timeout for the check is specified in the artifact for the CheckStep with name "Get the HttpWebResponse" at 15,000 milliseconds, and that is the only step that might run long. This means that it's the one to determine the duration of the check in case of timeout.

Open the artifacts from each of those dozen runs; they are all the newly-created XML files in the "Example_2..." directory under the "Artifacts" directory in the sample project.

In each artifact file, look under the CheckFailData element to see the failure data, including nested exceptions. Look under the CompleteCheckStepInfo element to see what step(s) failed and which ones were blocked. Note that a failed step can have a passed step as a child step, because failures propagate through parent steps up to the root.

If this check is repeated enough times, all four failure modes and success will all be represented.

Look in the solution, in the CheckMethods project, the source file for the methods used: Example_2_CheckOfWebPageBuiltToFailRandomly. Compare the hard-coded names of the Check.Step statements with the steps in the artifacts. Check where they match up.

More on creating and modifying checks

See the tutorial that comes with the Sample 1 download.

Review Questions

The answers are on page 213.

1) Try configuring a step with a timeout of A, and give the child step a timeout of B, with B > A. Which timeout takes precedence?
2) Why are stack traces parsed and broken up into distinct elements?
3) How would one code a negative test case?

Chapter 22
MetaAutomation Sample 2

Overview

See the section "How to Use the Samples" on pages 163-166 and the documentation included with the sample to get it running.

What Sample 2 Demonstrates

Communication between check components

If the check has more than one part (i.e., at least one sub-check) then the check components will run in different processes. The step results are integrated in the artifact and used as a step record for the next check run.

Things to Try

1. Try changing the name of a step in the code for a check, do a complete rebuild of the CheckMethods project and run it again. Note the step name is now changed in the artifact.

2. Try adding technology-facing steps (i.e., steps that have no child steps) for every product operation that might fail. Ask yourself which steps might fail at runtime, and for what reasons.

3. Verify that the business-facing steps (mostly, steps that have no parent steps) are described in terms of a business language or ubiquitous language that is meaningful to anyone and everyone on the product team, up to and including executives in the C-level suite.

4. Hard-code a failure (throw an exception) in check code, rebuild CheckMethods, and try

again. See how the exception is reported.

Creating and modifying checks

See the tutorial that comes with the Sample 1 download, and the Check Step Editor extension that is described with that tutorial.

Review Questions

The answers are on pages 213-214.

1) Why is it important that the names of the check steps be hard-coded?
2) Why is XML a good format for communicating across processes?

Chapter 23
MetaAutomation Sample 3

Overview

This sample includes an implementation of the Remote Testing Agent pattern (Guerra et al. 2014) and the Distributed Test Agent pattern (Farias et al. 2012).

See the section "How to Use the Samples" on pages 163-166, as well as the documentation included with the sample, to get it running. Sample 1 shows most of the new concepts, so it is recommended that you begin with it.

What Sample 3 demonstrates

Sample 3 does everything that Sample 2 does, and in addition it shows the following:

Distributed checks

Sample 2 is limited to one machine or OS instance.

Sample 3 can be distributed across any number of machines, OS instances, or tiers

on different machines or OS instances. This enables, for example, testing different tiers of a multi-tier app that necessarily must run on different hardware and/or a different operating system. This supports regressing quality for an "Internet of Things" application.

Please see Figure 43 on page 175 to see how the check runs across multiple tiers.

Scaled check runs

Sample 2 also scales across any number of machines.

In the sample implementation that is sample 2, the destination machines on which the checks will run are hard-coded. But, this can be extended so the automation finds the target machines at runtime for running the checks or sub-checks.

Things to Try

1. Edit the XML artifacts to change hard-coded destination machines for check components.
2. Try changing the destination machines at runtime. For a trivial example, set the destination machines at random after the CRL (Check Run Launch) is loaded and parsed into an XML document. For a more realistic implementation, the destination machine would come from an implementation of Precondition Pool or a job-running tool.
3. Examine the traces that are registered as events, and viewable in the Event Viewer, to see what the XML documents are that are passed around.

Creating and modifying checks

See the tutorial that comes with the Sample 1 download.

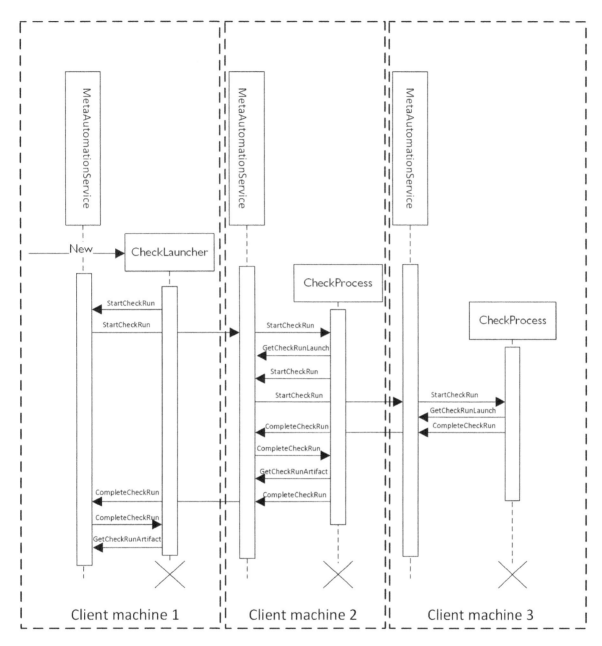

Fig. 43. Sequence diagram for Sample Check 2 in Sample 3.

Review Questions

The answers are on page 214.

1) Why are services needed on each machine, OS instance or hardware tier?
2) Why are the services XML-based?
3) What is the simplest way one would present each check run artifact as a web page, given the XSL presentation given in the solution?
4) Suppose the software system under development includes distributed services and an app with GUI on a mobile device. How would one run a check across multiple hardware tiers, including the mobile device?
5) In the source code provided, how would one customize the destination machine(s) on which the check will run, at runtime?

Section IV

Facing the Business

Chapter 24
Overview of Business-Facing Quality Automation

This section is about how the patterns of MetaAutomation fit together to deliver value to the business. Hierarchical Steps, Atomic Check and the other Check patterns, Parallel Run, Smart Retry, Automated Triage and Queryable Quality all work together to help the business ship software faster, at higher quality, higher quality confidence, and lower quality risk.

In this section the focus is on how Smart Retry and Automated Triage manifest to the business, but some parts of the Queryable Quality implementation – in the "Quality Portal" – will appear as well. For reference, see the pattern map on page 73.

This section will also reference the samples, so some experience running and playing with those will be valuable.

This section shows how all the patterns of MetaAutomation work together so quality automation helps the team be more productive.

Fig. 44. MetaAutomation makes developers more productive than previously possible.

Example Check Run

This hypothetical sample run shows 11 checks run as a set, across four automation clients, in Figure 45:

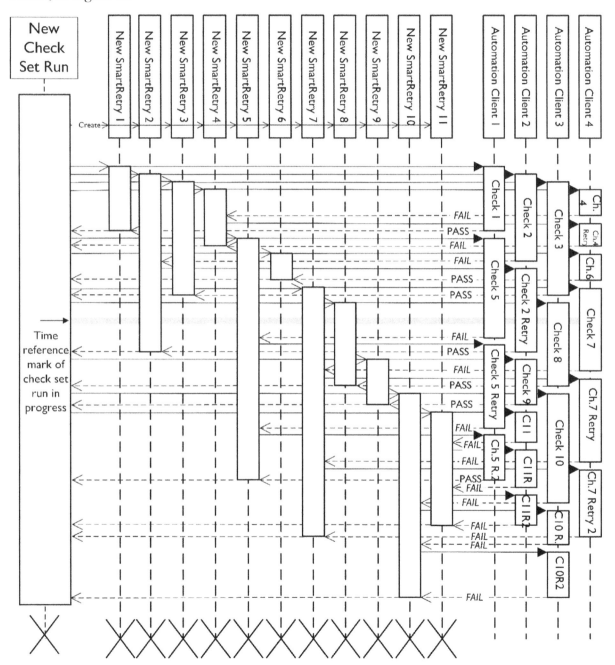

Fig. 45. Sequence diagram for the example check set run.

This sequence diagram shows time progress from the top to the bottom. The "time reference mark" at center left shows a moment in time during the check run. The view of the Quality Portal that is Figure 46 on page 183 shows this moment in time from the Quality Portal perspective.[144]

Check run in progress

This example uses the simpler version of Smart Retry. The simpler version of Smart Retry chooses whether to retry but makes that decision without considering root cause of given failure. The checks could be of a client GUI that is especially prone to failures from race conditions in the GUI and not enough opportunities for thread synchronization.

Increasingly cheap data storage gives the business opportunity to store all the data from check runs, so it can be queried from the portal for performance or reliability trends, subsets of certain checks that are reused, and many other things.

Below is a view of a model quality portal view of check runs ongoing and check run results, based on the Queryable Quality pattern,[145] with call-outs to interpret the view.

Figures 46-49 on pages 183-186 are based on a model of what an intranet site, which implements the check result part of the Queryable Quality pattern, might look like.

---

[144] The quality portal implementation suggested by the graphic is a simple design to show some values that the portal can bring to the team when full information on how the product is driven is available to them.

[145] See the Queryable Quality pattern on pages 155-158.

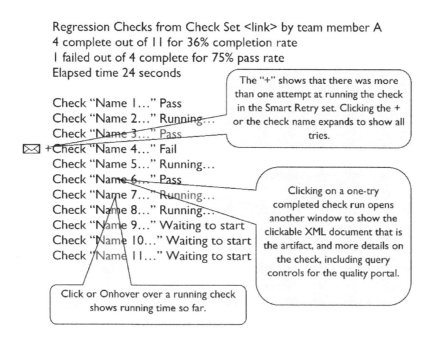

Fig. 46. Quality Portal view of check set run in progress.

The quality portal site might be implemented with AJAX (or something similar) to enable live or quasi-live updates from the server, so progress of the check set run could in theory be observed. Check run details are available as soon as any individual check run is complete.

Check run completed

Figure 47 below shows the same check run completed, and Figure 48 shows the same view expanded at each expandable node.

Figure 49 on page 186 adds information on linked bugs, and a hypothetical user interface for creating bugs linked to check failures. These bug links become important for sending notifications through the Automated Triage implementation.

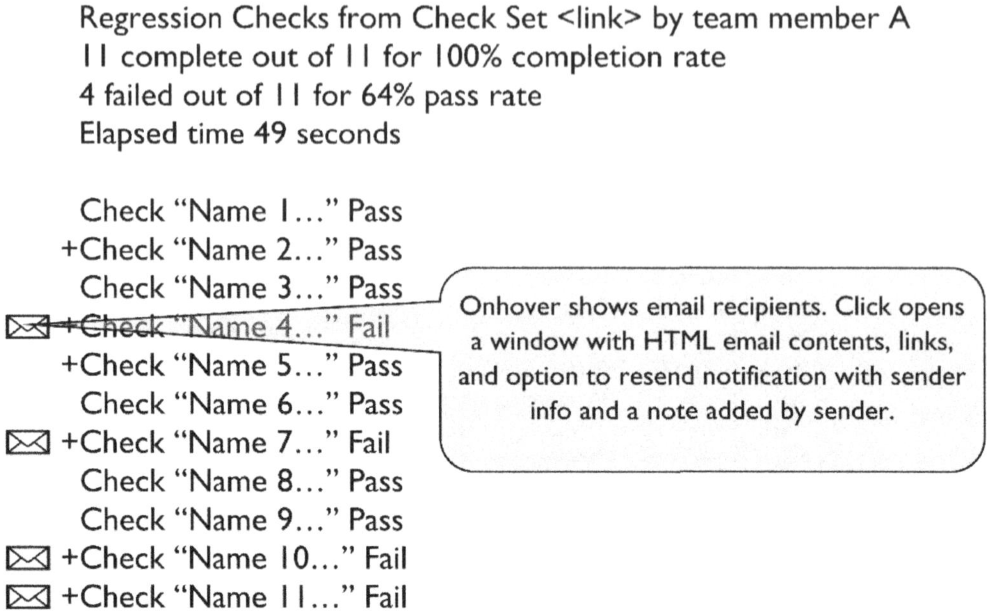

Regression Checks from Check Set <link> by team member A
11 complete out of 11 for 100% completion rate
4 failed out of 11 for 64% pass rate
Elapsed time 49 seconds

  Check "Name 1..." Pass
+Check "Name 2..." Pass
  Check "Name 3..." Pass
✉+Check "Name 4..." Fail
  +Check "Name 5..." Pass
  Check "Name 6..." Pass
✉ +Check "Name 7..." Fail
  Check "Name 8..." Pass
  Check "Name 9..." Pass
✉ +Check "Name 10..." Fail
✉ +Check "Name 11..." Fail

Onhover shows email recipients. Click opens a window with HTML email contents, links, and option to resend notification with sender info and a note added by sender.

Fig. 47. Quality Portal view of check set run complete.

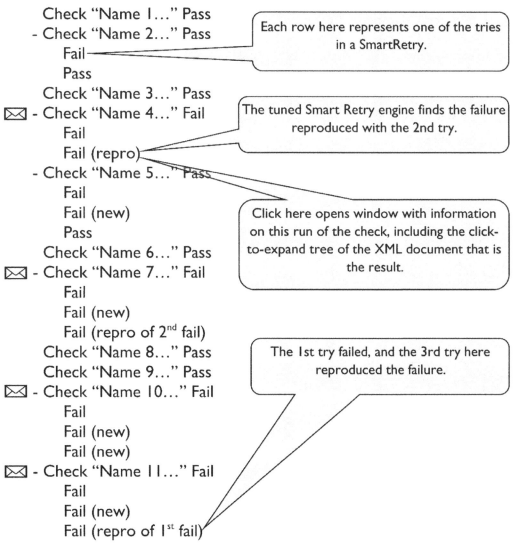

Fig. 48. Quality Portal expanded view of check set run complete.

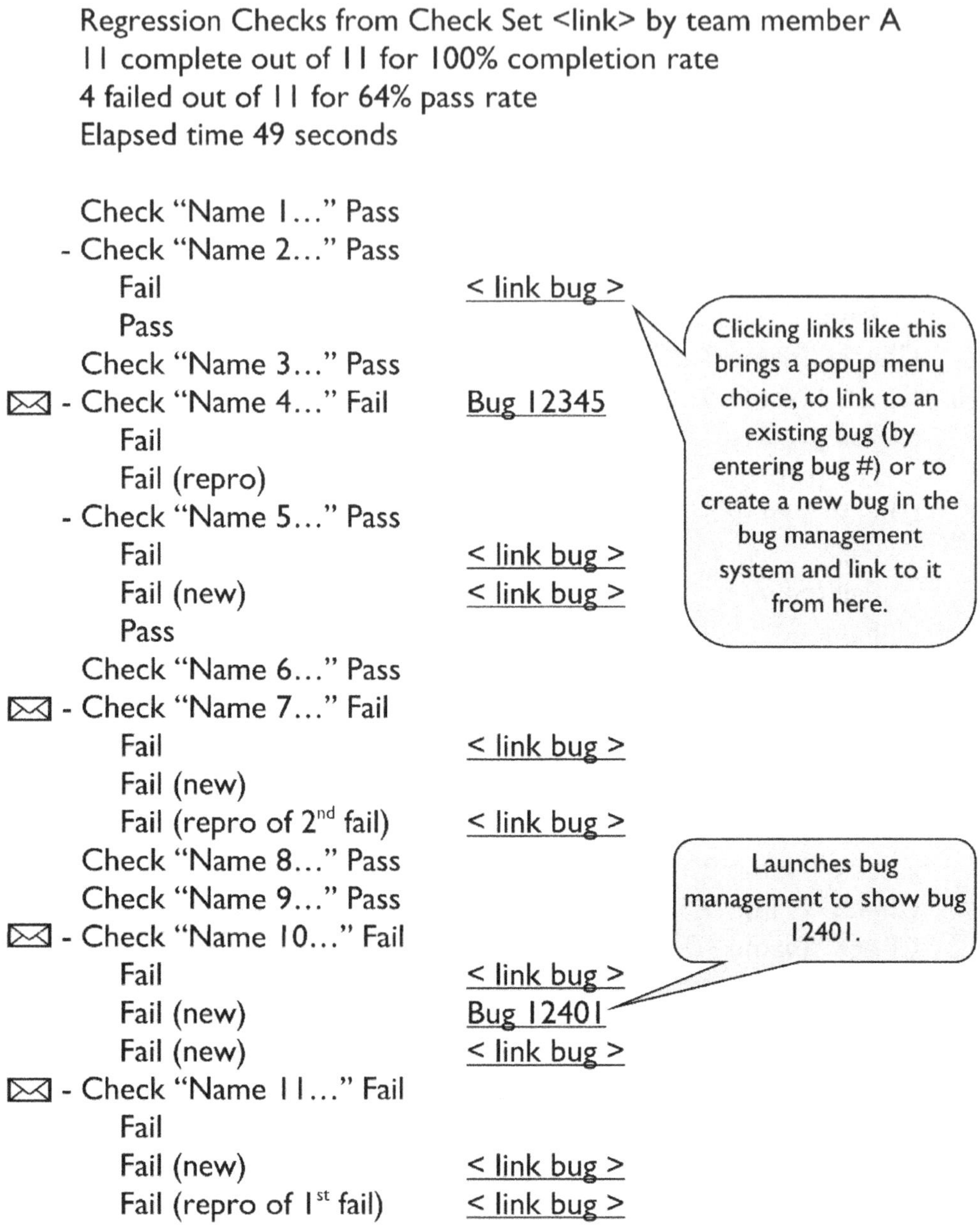

Regression Checks from Check Set <link> by team member A
11 complete out of 11 for 100% completion rate
4 failed out of 11 for 64% pass rate
Elapsed time 49 seconds

Check "Name 1..." Pass
- Check "Name 2..." Pass
    Fail   < link bug >
    Pass
Check "Name 3..." Pass
✉ - Check "Name 4..." Fail   Bug 12345
    Fail
    Fail (repro)
- Check "Name 5..." Pass
    Fail   < link bug >
    Fail (new)   < link bug >
    Pass
Check "Name 6..." Pass
✉ - Check "Name 7..." Fail
    Fail   < link bug >
    Fail (new)
    Fail (repro of 2nd fail)   < link bug >
Check "Name 8..." Pass
Check "Name 9..." Pass
✉ - Check "Name 10..." Fail
    Fail   < link bug >
    Fail (new)   Bug 12401
    Fail (new)   < link bug >
✉ - Check "Name 11..." Fail
    Fail
    Fail (new)   < link bug >
    Fail (repro of 1st fail)   < link bug >

> Clicking links like this brings a popup menu choice, to link to an existing bug (by entering bug #) or to create a new bug in the bug management system and link to it from here.

> Launches bug management to show bug 12401.

Fig. 49. Quality Portal view of check set run complete, with bug links.

Notifications could be sent on completion of runs of individual checks, just as bug links could be made available as well.

Try running any of the samples and viewing the results in an XML-supporting browser to see how the hierarchy of steps present a view from business-facing steps near the root of the hierarchy, and technology-facing steps at the leaf nodes. The samples are on pages 161-176.

Sending notifications

Figure 50 on the next page shows the activity for sending notifications. The "owner-only flag" is there for check runs on code images that are only visible to the developer that launched the check run, because in that case, only the owner of the changes needs to see the results.

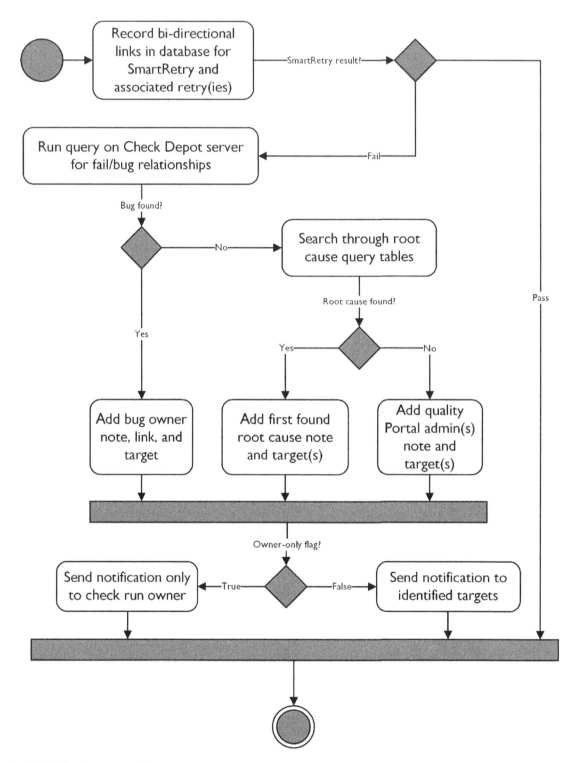

Fig. 50. Notification engine activity.

Linking to bugs

Figure 51 on the next page shows how Automated Triage might relate to people and objects of the business.

Note that although (as usual) it is humans who enter bugs[146] the bug relationships are reported and automatically duplicated as part of an automated triage implementation. A developer might therefore receive their targeted notification with, among other things, hard or tentative links to bugs.

The activity of the Notification Engine in Figure 51 directly relates to the activity diagram of Figure 50 above.

---

[146] However, future implementations might be sophisticated enough to create bugs that can only be handled by people.

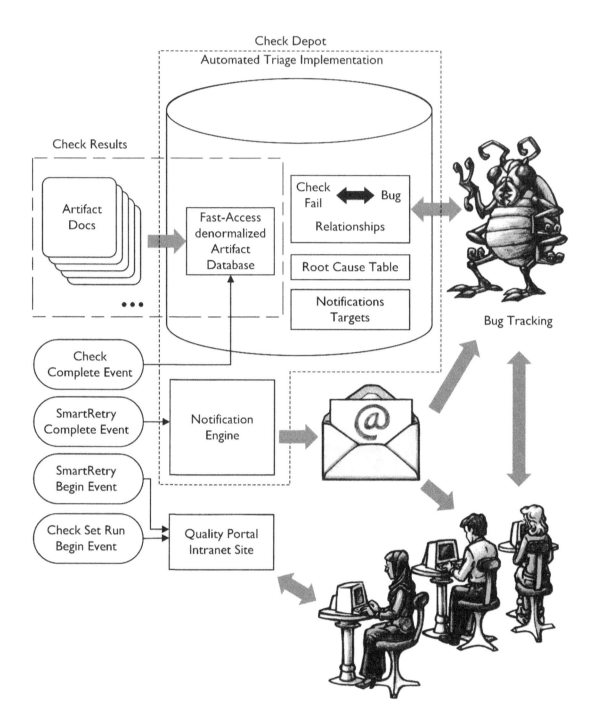

Fig. 51. Check depot relationship to the business.

Team impact

The impact map below in Figure 52 shows some of the ways in how the business – represented by team members of different roles – is affected by MetaAutomation.

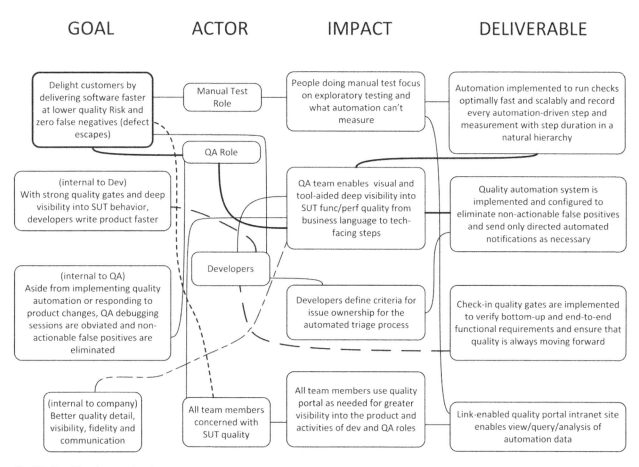

Fig. 52. The MetaAutomation impact map.

Review Questions

The answers are on pages 214-215.

1) Describe three changes in the team's approach to product quality that are necessary to realize the value of MetaAutomation.

2) Which patterns are represented in the sequence diagram on page 181?

3) What important aspect of persisting and communicating product behavior across the team is not represented in the diagrams of this section?

Section V

Appendices

Appendix 1
Atomic Checks from Existing Automation

Given Existing Intra-Test Dependencies

Here is a common anti-pattern of existing automation efforts for software quality: daisy-chaining tests, so the team must always run all the tests and always in the same order. The tests are set up in such a way that were they run individually or in a different set or order, they would not be expected to pass. Their value for measuring product quality would be suspect.

For purposes of this book, such a piece of automation is a single check, and not a good one. It is slow and brittle, and expensive to support. Analysis of any failure in such a check is going to be expensive, whether root cause is a failure in the SUT or in the check itself, due to a time-consuming debug session to find out what is going on.

Depending on context and resources, it might or might not be worth the investment to refactor the tested properties of the SUT, i.e., the quality-measuring value of this original automated test (or test set) into a set of atomic checks. The cost and the opportunity are both significant. The rest of this section assumes that the team decides to go ahead with the refactoring.

The first step is to break the original automation into smaller checks, each one with a target that is easily verifiable, stable, and important to the business logic of the SUT.

The atomicity of these checks — meaning, the checks can't be any simpler while still meeting the requirements of the Atomic Check pattern — might appear at first to conflict with the overall performance of the set of checks. For example, a set of checks might depend on a document that is updated by the checks, or the set might depend on an expensive application initialization. To make many checks out of the long original piece of automation, a certain state (of the document, database, or app) is assumed at certain points, and if the automation were broken into smaller pieces, that state would have to be managed or imaged for reuse. However, when the refactoring is complete, faster-quality measurements and communication will be possible, through flexible check selection and scaling.

Consider adding to the Precondition Pool implementation to enable the needed state to be managed offline, so the smaller checks can still run quickly, independently, and with the required state at check begin.

Remove less-important or flaky verifications. The costs of leaving these in (frequent failures, untested product, and performance and maintenance issues) might exceed the value of the verifications, and it certainly interferes with the atomicity of the checks.

Ensure that the checks can run independently of each other, so the check run can scale with resources.

Consider adding to the artifacts or rebuild the artifact generation to follow the Atomic Check pattern. The sample provided with this book may help with this, and it will make the results of the checks much more compact and actionable, and even subject to automated operations as with the Smart Retry pattern and Automated Triage.

If the original test depended on manual test cases, consider making the checks independent of the original test cases. The original test cases always had quality measurement value in being run manually. But with independent checks, that value can now be made explicit, and with a complete implementation of the Atomic Check pattern, the checks can be self-documenting as well.

Given Existing Automation in a Script Language

See Appendix 2 "Language Choices" on pages 197-200 for an explanation on the limitations of scripting languages.

Some options for the team to consider:

•   Many tools will take the script code and translate it into a different language. The team can then refactor the checks and the code to reflect the Atomic Check pattern to get the benefits of applying that pattern.

•   The team could refactor the existing checks into shorter ones that can be distributed and therefore run faster.

•   The team could rewrite the checks incrementally and continue running existing checks until they are rewritten or refactored, as long as they are worth the cost of maintaining them.

•   Consider the steps in the previous section to refactor the checks into ones that can deliver on the promise of faster, more effective communication around the team on product quality.

Appendix 2
Language Choices

The patterns of MetaAutomation are language-independent, but some languages are not powerful enough to implement all the patterns at the highest level of automation.

People writing code to automate a procedure sometimes call it a "script," but that label comes from the procedural nature of the automation rather than a property of the language used. Automation code does not have to be a script language.

The table on the next page shows language properties and suggested languages that will work, and some languages that will not work for each property.

Property	Application of Property	Sample languages	Languages that will *not* support the property
OO class derivation	Custom exception class or classes, to carry actionable information at failed checks	C#, Java, C++	Perl Javascript (sort of)
OO life cycle control	Automatic marking of conclusion of check steps	C#, Java (recent versions), Python	Ruby Javascript
Strong typing	Exception handling for check failure messages	C#, Java	Ruby, Python, Javascript
Reflection	Helps in connecting the check steps with artifacts	C#, Java	C++, Javascript
Distributed run	Parallel Run pattern, Smart Retry pattern	C#, Java	Any script will need an interpreter to be distributed as well, and performance and versioning may be problematic
Business Continuity	Planning for the possibility of personnel change on short notice	The same language that the product is written in, or C#, Java, other standard languages with business support	Any small-market-share language
Multi-threading and synchronization	Managing parallel check runs, timeouts and other error conditions	C#, Java, C++	Ruby, Python, Javascript

For example, C# will work when driving Selenium or client JavaScript because it is sufficiently powerful to handle exceptions, lifecycle management, distribution, etc. for a complete system that implements any or all the patterns in MetaAutomation. However, Ruby will not.

For the MetaAutomation samples, I chose C# because it has better declarative syntax capabilities, better XML support, better overall design, and stronger support than Java. If platform-independence is a requirement for your project's test environment, consider the Mono project for .Net. If the quality project needs platforms or features not supported by .Net and Mono, then Java or some other language that runs on the Java Virtual Machine platform may be the best choice.

Script languages, e.g., Python or Ruby, have the very expensive tendency to defer errors to runtime, rather than at compile-time. With distributed systems, this means that some errors are deferred to post-distribution time. The inevitable cycles of discovering failures due to test bugs, fixing them, and trying again, will take longer without a strongly typed compiled language. Use of a scripting language will scale to support MetaAutomation with difficulty, or not at all.

This error-deferment problem is reported in the 2017 paper by Jiang et al. where test script defects account for 11.64% or 46.71% (for two data sets) of causes for manual analysis. In the same paper, it is reported that

> *On average, testers are requested to analyze 192 and 317 test alarms per day… (Jiang et al. 2017)*

Since many such errors are reported immediately by a compiler, in those cases alone, cost would be much lower with a compiled language. As I like to say, the compiler is your friend.

In most cases, you will write code in the same language as the product. If for some reason that is not an option, use a language that will give you the full power of the MetaAutomation pattern language: C#, C++, or Java.

Writing check code in a language that is different from product code may lose information from the SUT if a language transition happens as part of a stack-based call in the same process, especially if an exception is thrown across the inter-language boundary or is stopped by the boundary. In addition, if there are script layers or tools between the automation code and product code, there are potential points of failure and/or obfuscation between the automation code and the product. Maintenance becomes more difficult because the added layer of complexity presents potential points of failure and issues that must be verified manually to address the question "Does this automation do what we think it does with the product?" Therefore, writing automation in the same language as the product typically works best.

Appendix 3
Coding Styles

Quality automation code is very important to the business and is worthy of care and attention. With MetaAutomation, communication around the larger team, and decisions on when, whether, or how often to ship, all depend on that code.

As Elisabeth Hendrickson wrote

> It is tempting for organizations to treat infrastructure code as somehow inferior to production code. 'It's just scripts,' they say. 'We don't need to put seasoned engineers on it.' However, what I've seen is that the infrastructure code — that includes build and CI scripts as well as tests and test frameworks — is the foundation on which the rest of the code is built. If the infrastructure code is not treated with the same care as production code, then everything is built on a shaky foundation. (Hendrickson 2016)

In the simple case that the automation code is in the same language as the product code, then the product code standards are the place to start for automation code standards. However, there are significant differences between what is best for product code vs. automation code, especially automation code that neither ships to end-user environments nor effects end-user experiences directly.

From the security perspective, automation code can be more liberal with exception information than product code because check code is internal or used with testing in production (TIP). Unlike with product code, confidentiality is not an issue, and performance is less important.

Automation code has much less of a performance constraint, too, so it can do increasingly risky things than product code can be allowed.

On use of code comments, see "Replace code comments with something better" on page 47.

The three samples in this book (pages 161-176) show my personal take on what the automation code to drive the SUT could look like. It is sophisticated and capable code, but there is a good chance that improvements can be made. See the section "Future Patterns for MetaAutomation" on pages 159-160 to see how to contribute.

Appendix 4
Unit Tests

Unit tests are about testing a unit, e.g., a class, assembly, or a library without any dependencies (or, dependencies faked or stubbed out).

Unit tests are out of scope for this book for two reasons:

1. They are developer-facing. Unit test results mean little or nothing to anyone else on the team.
2. Aside from a few algorithm-specific units, they do not relate to business or functional requirements.[147]

In my work I have seen more than a few unit tests that depended on the implementation in the SUT so closely, a refactor of the product method would break the unit test. A common rationale for unit tests – that they enable safe refactoring of a method – might be false in those cases.

System tests — part of the focus of this book — have more meaning for software quality. As James Coplien wrote

> *Most software failures come from the interactions between objects rather than being a property of an object or method in isolation. (Coplien 2018)*

---

[147] E.g., a unit might have compression or encoding algorithms that link to a functional requirement.

Wayne Roseberry notes in his paper from PNSQC 2016

> *It is also the case that integration points are one of the most common sources of bugs... It is very common that all unit tests will pass splendidly, only to release code that fails because of something unexpected at an integration point. (Roseberry 2016)*

This book shows a way of doing system tests with automation faster than before and with better, more informative results, so unit tests are less important.

Answers to Review Questions

Section I: Introduction to MetaAutomation

Chapter 3: Fixing "Test Automation"

The questions are on page 35.

1) Quality automation can bring, for example, these values to the business:
   a) It can run independently of geography.
   b) It can run at all hours.
   c) It can scale with added computing resources, much more cheaply, easily, and effectively than hiring more people.
   d) It can reliably ensure that measured aspects of product quality are still adequate (or, if not, start a notification workflow to alert people).
   e) It does not get tired, bored, or distracted.

2) People doing manual testing, with or without a script, have intelligence — analytical and emotional — and the powers of observation to notice and characterize quality issues that otherwise might never come to the attention of the team.

3) Automating a process is about achieving what people might do, but doing it with machines (e.g., computing machines) automatically, faster, better, and more cheaply. By linguistic relativity, "test automation" implies that it is "test" being automated, which mostly, it is not; the human intelligence, creativity, resilience, powers of observation, and quality discussions that are part of the process known as "test" cannot be automated. What *can* be automated is quality measurements, simple rule-based decisions, and communications; hence the phrase "quality automation."

4) Depending on your perspective, the most basic value could be
   a) The ability to ship software faster and at higher quality confidence

b) efficient communication to everybody on the product team who cares, either push (e.g., email) or pull (e.g., through an intranet site), with detailed information on how the SUT is driven, what is measured, the results, and timing of every step.

c) A more powerful realization of what quality automation can do for the team, to enable the quality team.

5) MetaAutomation brings quality automation to DevOps, with vastly improved reliability, timeliness, transparency, confidence in quality and knowledge of exactly what is measured.

6) The manual testing role is more productive and less tedious if it can concentrate on what the manual testing role does well. The need for manual testers to do tedious manual scripts goes away, and testers can concentrate on what they do well: aspects of product quality that are difficult or impossible to automate. For example, manual test is needed for web site layout, usability, discoverability, and some aspects of performance and things that the manual testing role must find and characterize. MetaAutomation helps by reporting with precision, accuracy, and high trustworthiness the important behaviors of the product, in a way that manual testers can see in the intranet and therefore skip tedious and easy-to-measure verifications.

Chapter 5: Paradigm Shift One: Bring Value from All Functional Quality Data

The questions are on page 50.

1) The meme that test is all about finding bugs implies that, if a check finds no bugs (as with a green bubble pass) then nobody cares other than the fact that the check passed.

2) Logs are the perfect tool for monitoring instrumentation or a software product because they are very simple and lightweight: they just record some information and a timestamp, and they are done. For code that drives a procedure in the SUT, performance is much less important, but context of an operation (and, performance of that operation) is very important. Logs drop all context by design (although some of that context can sometimes be restored through identifiers in a log statement).

3) Some advantages include:

a) Performance can be measured and reported at every step, so perf data is much more complete and there is no need for special code just for perf testing.

b) Anyone on the team who cares about SUT quality can see exactly what is going on with the quality automation.

c) On a check fail, a retry might be done[148] or a notification might be efficiently directed[149] based on detailed information on failure root cause.

---

[148] See the Smart Retry pattern on pages 141-150.

[149] See the Automated Triage pattern on pages 151-154.

d) Quality data is highly detailed and enables analysis over time to see trends in performance or correctness.

e) SUT quality is highly measurable, lowering quality risk and raising confidence in shipping the product.

f) On a check fail, assuming a repeatable check that ran to completion at least once before, the failed steps leading up the hierarchy are reported as are the steps that are blocked by the failure. Blocked steps show what the check was "trying" to do and allows better assessment of quality risk related to the unmeasured, blocked steps in case of a persistent failure.

Chapter 6: Paradigm Shift Two: Bring Value to the Whole Team

The questions are on page 57.

1) Using automation to record all details of driving and measuring the SUT and putting it up on the intranet quality portal in a format that is accessible to anyone in the business, raises visibility of exactly what the SUT is doing as part of the quality automation. More transparency means more efficient communication and collaboration.

2) Manual testers know exactly what has been measured on the SUT, so they can test around that rather than repeating it.

There is little or no need of supporting manual test scripts.

3) With MetaAutomation, QA becomes the hub of communication around software quality and behaviors of the SUT. QA builds the tools that enable developers to ship higher-quality software faster, enable manual testers to be more efficient and less burdened with tedium, give managers and leads high visibility into dev, test, and QA productivity, and allow accountants to have a detailed and trustworthy picture of product quality.

Chapter 7: Paradigm Shift Three: Bring Value from the Whole Ecosystem

The questions are on page 66.

1) Modern software applications are internet-enabled. Many of them are intensively interconnected. For such applications, testing in isolation from dependencies risks changing important behaviors or even removing the most important functionality. Quality risk happens when important functionality — including handling error conditions or unexpected information — is not tested until later, when issues that need code changes in the SUT cause, in turn, new costs and quality risks.

2) Some advantages:

a) The less-dependent layers of the SUT are less likely to go through design changes in a way that requires changes in the automation code to keep up.

b) In case of check fail, the Information from the SUT is richer if it includes an exception and stack trace, rather than information about GUI elements.

c) Automation without a GUI layer will run faster

d) Bugs that only appear in a GUI layer are low-risk to fix, because the business-logic or services layer of the SUT is not affected.

3) Two reasons that external dependencies are left out of quality checks are speed and reliability. The Atomic Check, Precondition Pool and Parallel Run patterns take care of the speed issue. The reliability issue is covered by the Hierarchical Steps, Atomic Check, and Smart Retry patterns.

Section II: The Pattern Language

Chapter 8: Pattern Language: MetaAutomation

The questions are on page 76.

1) There are strong and ordered dependencies between the patterns, and MetaAutomation spans a well-defined problem space.
2) The starting pattern for MetaAutomation is Hierarchical Steps, although this pattern is implemented as part of the Atomic Check pattern.
3) Quality automation is the problem space between driving the SUT with automation for quality measurements, on the technical side, and addressing the people and processes that depend on quality information — the customers — on the business side. For example, DevOps is a customer of the quality automation problem space because it needs to know whether a given build of the SUT is of enough functional quality to be promoted. Developers are customers of the quality automation space because they need to know of functional correctness quickly and often. MetaAutomation is a pattern language that shows an optimal implementation of quality automation with a focus on a fast and repeatable answer to the question "does the system do what we need it to do?" and is a living and growing pattern language as well.

Chapter 9: Software Pattern: Prioritized Requirements

The questions are on page 83.

1) Here are three reasons that business requirements are important:
   a) They are outward-facing towards the needs of the end-users, i.e., independent of design or implementation.
   b) They can be prioritized according to end-user needs, independent of design or implementation of the SUT.
   c) Knowledge of the business requirements is important context for the functional requirements that relate to them. In case of changes to design or features, knowing the business requirements keeps functional requirements grounded in the end-user's needs.
2) If business requirements are not recorded and available to the team, these risks could result:
   a) Team members might disagree on how the product should behave, either overtly or silently. Worse, they might think that they understand, but they do not. This could cause inconsistency across the product or late changes to try to correct.

b) There is extra cost, confusion, ignorance and/or dissonance in bringing on new team members.

Chapter 10: MetaAutomation Pattern: Hierarchical Steps

The questions are on page 98.

1) Some examples of step hierarchies from common daily activities:

a) Following driving directions

i) If the first high-level step is "Get on Big Highway going south," the child steps might be "Turn the car on," "Go to the main street," "Take a left onto the main street," and "Turn at the highway entrance to go south." Child steps of "Go to the main street" might be "Pull forward far enough to see if there is traffic," "wait as needed for traffic," "Take a left turn," "Proceed to the stop sign," "Take a left," and "enter Big Highway south."

ii) In a list hierarchy, this would look like the following:

(1)   Get on Big Highway going south

   (a) Turn the car on

   (b) Go to the main street

     (i) Pull forward far enough to see if there is traffic

     (ii) Wait as needed for traffic

   (c) Take a left turn

   (d) Proceed to Stop sign

   (e) Take a left

   (f) Turn at the highway entrance to go south

b) Baking a chocolate cake with icing

c) Preparing a tax return

d) Fixing a bike

e) Brushing your teeth

f) Buying espresso

g) Emailing a friend

2) Here are two essential differences:

a) Each log statement stands alone, by default, and reports some bit of information in a highly performant way. When driving the SUT for quality measurements, the procedure is important for SUT behavior, so information about beginning and ending of each step, and the relationship between the steps, is very important.

b) Quality automation code does not ship or impact end-users directly, so performant code is not nearly as important.

3) Extensible Markup Language (XML) is well established as a W3C[150] standard, and has full schema (XSD), transform (XSLT), query (XPath, XQuery) capabilities.[151] As a meta-language, it is very flexible and powerful tool for working with hierarchical data. XML is highly compressible and is implicitly compressed for many databases and communication channels. By contrast, JavaScript Object Notation (JSON) is

---

[150] The World Wide Web consortium.

[151] The code samples of this book use XSD, XSLT, and XPath.

simpler but less general since it was designed around the JavaScript language. It lacks an established standard schema (at publication date), and the same is true of query and transform capabilities, so the stability risk is greater than with XML.

Chapter 11: MetaAutomation Pattern: Atomic Check

The questions are on page 119.

1) Artifacts are structured and detailed, with self-documenting hierarchical steps.

2) It is a requirement that all atomic checks be independent of each other at runtime. It is ideal that all atomic checks are independent of each other in terms of what they measure, but in practice this is not possible due to the complexity of some functional requirements. It is inevitable that a given flaw in the SUT (or the environment) might cause more than one check to fail.

3) The Setup and Teardown patterns move some operations of the check out-of-line, so the artifacts cannot be recorded in the same structure. For any failures to be highly actionable in a consistent way, one data structure must have all results.

4) Itemizing business requirements separately from the functional requirements that a check measures gives two advantages: first, requirements "drift" is prevented because the rationale for any functional requirement is clearly understood from the customer point of view, and so recorded, and second, the functional requirements can be correctly prioritized for implementation and measurement according to the business requirements.

Chapter 12: MetaAutomation Pattern: Event-Driven Check

The questions are on page 124.

1) The SUT in the test environment must subscribe to events that are under control of the quality automation. At check runtime, the automation triggers the events.

2) Checks that the team depends on to keep quality going forward must be at least fairly reliable (depending on circumstances, about 80% at least). For product properties that depend on external events, there might be no other way to create reliably repeatable checks for that property. The risk of changing dependencies is relatively small because the events are simpler than requests of external services.

Chapter 13: MetaAutomation Pattern: Extension Check

The questions are on page 128.

1) The behavior measured by Extension Check is not deterministic, so results from such a check might not be deterministic either. The Smart Retry pattern does not apply to Extension Check.

2) Performance criteria for the SUT could change for many reasons, depending on the complexity of the process that

decided what the precise performance criteria are. A criterion for gated check-in, however, must be stable so that what passed for one developer does not break another one. The risk of using performance criteria is that an unexpected failure might block one developer due to an issue not related to what the developer's change set is about.

Chapter 14: MetaAutomation Pattern: Precondition Pool

The questions are on page 134.

1) Any operations that might be done in a traditional Setup or Teardown pattern implementation that can also be done out-of-line or in a different process, are put in a Precondition Pool implementation. A Precondition Pool implementation manages any failures separately from the check run, so Precondition Pool does not add to overhead or complexity of the check run.[152]

2) Precondition Pool simplifies the checks giving these three advantages: they run faster, with fewer potential points of failure, and simpler results. The pool handles any failures in setting up the preconditions, so such failures do not complicate the check run.

Chapter 15: MetaAutomation Pattern: Parallel Run

The questions are on page 140.

1) Atomic Check requires that all checks be runtime independent of each other, so they can run in any set or any order. This is necessary to scale the check runs with resources. The "atomic" aspect of the checks also ensures that the checks are as short and simple as possible, helping scale as well.

2) Parallel Run enables scale of quality automation, which in turn enables reliability and timeliness of the quality measurements. This gives in turn the confidence to move forward with product development and shipping.

Chapter 16: MetaAutomation Pattern: Smart Retry

The questions are on page 150.

1) Smart Retry can be configured to either retry every time on failure or retry depending on the failure root cause shown in the check artifact. Smart Retry will also show if a specific root cause for failure was reproduced in a second try, or if a different failure occurred, try a third time (depending again on configuration). In either case, the check run failure is recorded in a complete artifact for future analysis or reporting as needed.

2) The Hierarchical Steps pattern, applied with Atomic Check, give detailed data on driving and measuring the SUT in a

---

[152] The overhead of Precondition Pool implementations might slow a check run, but only if the pool resources are used up and must be replenished, and hardly more than a Setup/Teardown would do.

simple, scalable check, which is independent of all other checks.

Chapter 17: MetaAutomation Pattern: Automated Triage

The questions are on page 154.

1) Automated Triage sends notifications on an as-needed basis and to a targeted audience. When QA has configured the system correctly according to who owns what areas of code, developers who receive a notification about a check failure have a high degree of confidence that it is an action item for them to address. There is less randomization of engineers, a proper priority in context-switching as needed to address failures, and less deluging engineers with information that might end up ignored. Developers can therefore respond faster to fix issues, and keep development moving forward.

2) Automated Triage also links to check results on a Queryable Quality implementation on the intranet, for anyone with the will and permissions to see, and (optionally) for anyone to configure and launch check runs. Queryable Quality can also include links to communicate with people on the team who are targets of any notifications sent in response to a check fail.

Chapter 18: MetaAutomation Pattern: Queryable Quality

The questions are on page 158.

1) An implementation of Atomic Check persists these aspects of each check run to make them available to Queryable Quality:
   a) The complete hierarchy of check steps is presented
   b) Every check step has status of pass, fail, or blocked
   c) The timing of each check step, including the high-level business-facing steps and the low-level technology-facing steps
   d) Whether a check failure was a one-off failure, or whether it was reproduced exactly

2) The artifacts of a check run are short, simple, structured, and strongly typed, with self-documenting steps, so analysis is simpler, more efficient, and more useful than if the checks were more complex or unstructured.

3) A quality portal makes all the data from quality automation available across the team. For the part of SOX compliance concerned with the functional quality and performance of the software that a company has produced or is working on, this transparency is key. This highly detailed information on the product is available for detailed and very trustworthy evaluations of software under development.

Section III: Sample Solutions

Chapter 20: How to Use the Samples

The questions are on page 166.

1) The samples show how to write check code that both drives the software product under test *and* documents itself. At runtime, the code of the check steps puts data for the step inside an XML Element in the artifact that the check run generates. Every time the check runs, it documents itself!

2) The code that drives the software product defines check steps. Check steps can have zero or more check steps as children. If the check code includes a method call, that method becomes reported as another check step. The order of check steps is preserved and reported in the same order and hierarchy as the code and the execution of the code, including method calls, forming an ordered-tree hierarchy.

3) If a given check has run without fail far enough to execute step "StepA," then StepA and all previous steps, and their hierarchy, are documented in the check run artifact. If the next run of that check executes the same steps in the same hierarchy, either until check fail or until check pass, the record of those steps is preserved whether or not the steps are executed. If the check fails while the record of further steps is preserved, they are recorded as "blocked."

Chapter 21: MetaAutomation Sample 1

The questions are on page 170.

1) Every step with a timeout will follow through with that timeout, no matter what happens in child steps. Therefore, the timeout configured for step A may fail the check with a timeout.

2) Stack traces are easier and more robust to compare as part of a quality automation system when they have been parsed into segments to represent the stack levels.

3) A negative check expects a failure with certain characteristics within the steps of the check, but in case of that expected failure, the check will succeed with all steps self-documenting in the code as usual. Therefore, the expected failure must be measured and contained within a check step. In case of an expected exception, the exception must be caught in the step, but if the expected exception does not happen, that step must fail. See Example 3 in Sample 1 for a simple implementation of this.

Chapter 22: MetaAutomation Sample 2

The questions are on page 172.

1) The step names are hard-coded because they need to be both stable and unique: stable because the artifacts of the check runs, which contain those names as queryable properties in the artifact data, must be meaningful across the time span for which the checks are being run on

the system under test, i.e., across most of all of the SDLC or multiple SDLC's, and unique for similar reasons. Custom data for any check step can always be injected with another XML element. This also means that if for some reason, e.g., a conscious change in team language or product marketing, a step name is

Chapter 23: MetaAutomation Sample 3

The questions are on page 176.

1) The services provide listeners to respond to requests to drive and measure the product code, independently of the product code itself.
2) The services are XML based for platform-independence, but also because XML is a standard of the W3C (reference: World Wide Web Consortium) with supporting standard technologies, e.g., XSD schema and XSL transforms.
3) Copy the XSLT stylesheet in the "ReferenceDocuments" folder of the solution into the file directory where artifacts are placed as XML files and put code in the artifacts to use the XSL presentation. The first two lines of the XML artifact file will then look like the two lines here, with the second line showing the stylesheet file:

Section IV: Facing the Business

Chapter 24: Overview of Business-Facing Quality Automation

The questions are on page 192.

1) Here are some changes in how a team approaches quality that are necessary preconditions for realizing the benefits of MetaAutomation:

changed, that change is easy to track, or query as needed in the source code control system used by the team.
2) XML is text-based and a well-established standard metalanguage, with established and implemented standards for schemas, transforms, and queries.

a) `<?xml version="1.0" encoding="utf-8"?>`
b) `<?xml-stylesheet href='CheckRunArtifact.xsl' type='text/xsl' ?>`
4) Run the XML-based MetaAutomationService or the equivalent on the target device or emulation and use the service to launch the device app without the GUI, calling the business-logic layers of the app directly from check code. This can run as a sub-check, with the higher-level check calling services directly and measuring responses, so the entire system (less the GUI of the app) is measured in one check.
5) At the beginning of a check launch, just after the artifact from the last run of the check is loaded in memory, update the destination machines as desired.

a) The team must discover and itemize business requirements, prioritize them, and then use that to prioritize the testable functional requirements.

b) The functional requirements, not test cases, are used to guide quality automation.

c) The team must not chain tests; checks are atomic and completely independent of each other at check run time.

d) The team implements checks including hierarchical self-documented steps, so that a check run creates pure-data artifacts that reflect check steps in a stable, ordered hierarchy.

2) These MetaAutomation patterns are represented in the sequence diagram on page 181:

a) Hierarchical Steps is represented indirectly because it enables the Smart Retry pattern.

b) Atomic Check is represented because it enables checks to be simple, quick, and independent of each other.

c) Parallel Run is shown because the checks are running in parallel across different environments.

d) Smart Retry is represented with the retries of failed check. It is the simpler version of Smart Retry that does retries that are not contingent on root cause of the failure, or at least, a Smart Retry that retries all of the check failures shown.

3) There is no diagram showing directly how the Hierarchical Steps pattern provides business-facing steps near the root and enables drill-down to the technology-facing leaf steps. See the samples for this and view the check results in a browser that enables drill-down into the XML. For example, the Chrome or Edge browsers support this view.

Glossary

Actionability

The property of how well a piece of information translates to an action item, from the perspective of the person on the team who receives the information.

See Actionable.

Actionable

A work item for a person on the software team that has clear business value for the software product, and clear next steps, is actionable. For example, a bug assigned to a developer with clear root cause and steps to reproduce the problem is actionable, whether the bug is ultimately fixed or not.

See Actionability

Analytics

In the context of product quality, analytics is the practice of measuring product quality, performance, profiling how the product is used, etc. from product instrumentation and server logs and as the product is exercised by the end-user.

See Synthetics.

Antipattern

An antipattern is a common pattern of behavior in response to a recurring problem that has a significant negative attribute. For example, the Chained Tests pattern recorded by Meszaros is an antipattern in the sense that chaining automated tests has significant negative impacts on efficiency, value of data generated, and the scalability of the check runs with computing resources (Meszaros 2007, p. 454).

API

Application Programming Interface.

Artifact

An artifact is information generated as part of the software development process that is not part of the software product.

For the context of this book, an artifact is information on quality of the SUT that the automation measures and persists while executing a bounded and repeatable automated check.

For the context of the software samples of this book, an artifact is the XML file that is generated by each run of each check and serves as a reference for the next run of the same check. As the samples are implemented, the check will not run without such a reference. This is illustrated with Figure 42 on page 165.

Atom

(For the context of this book) An object, measurement or piece of information that cannot be reduced in size without changing the nature of the object or information.

Atomic Check

Atomic Check (capitalized) is the name of an important pattern of MetaAutomation.

An atomic check (lower case) verifies the linked functional requirement using as few steps as possible in driving the SUT. To avoid the risk of measuring the SUT out of context, all dependencies are in place. The "atomic" part of the check is that it can't be made any simpler.

See Check.

Atomic Step

An atomic step is a step in a procedure that, from the perspective of non-product code or code owned by the QA role, cannot divide into smaller non-trivial steps (i.e., steps that could fail). In the hierarchy of steps for an Atomic Check, the atomic steps are also leaf steps because, being indivisible, they have no child steps.

Atomicity

The property of being as small as possible while keeping the essential value.

Automated Checking

When it is automation that drives the checks.

With automated checking, fail events can only come from either the SUT or quality code.

Contrast with Manual Testing.

See Check.

Automated Verification

A procedure in code that, when executed, reports at least a result of pass, or fail. A check consists of one or more automated verifications.

See Check.

Bottom-Up Testing

Bottom-up testing is quality measurement that drives and measures less-dependent components of the software product first and integrates with dependent services if applicable and possible. Usually this involves automation, so is a type of automated checking for purposes of this book. The parts of the system that are lowest-risk and lowest-cost respecting changes to code, e.g., the GUI or web pages, are tested last.

Bug

A quality issue of concern to the product team, usually specific to the product, but can concern quality automation as well.

For any significant application, people record and track bugs. Many bugs are fixed, but if testing is done well, there will be so many bugs recorded that there will not be enough resources to fix ones that are lower priority. Bugs that are not fixed have value as measures of product quality, and as records of product behavior that are known to and triaged by the team to decide whether they get fixed. Issues that end-users experience with the product are less expensive and less risky to the team if a bug that records that issue is already known to the team.

For purposes of this book, a check failure is not the same thing as a bug and might nor might not be correlated with a bug.

Business

For the context of this book, "business" or "the business" refers to the higher-level purpose of the software project or system or organized team of people. This could be, e.g., a for-profit business, or an embedded software system, or an open-source software project. "The business" could therefore be the equivalent of "the high-level method that the team uses to deliver the greatest value."

Business Requirement

A business requirement is a required characteristic of the SUT, defined in an implementation-independent way and from a customer or business perspective. Business requirements link to functional requirements.

See Atomic Check.

See Functional Requirement.

Check

(noun) A type of test that is not intended to be run manually, and which has specific, defined and well-understood verifications as criteria for success. A check has one or more automated verifications.

(noun) A procedure and rule that is automated or intended to be automated to reveal information about product quality; or in case of test-driven development (see TDD) something that functions as a measure of whether implementation is complete.

(noun) A procedure that, when executed, has at least a result of pass or fail.

(verb) To execute such a procedure.

In the context of this book, checks do not include the use of synthetic techniques.

See Automated Verification.

See Checking.

See Synthetics.

See Test.

Check Run

An instance of a check run or run of a set of checks.

See Check.

Checking

Running one or more checks or automated verifications.

When people test, they can observe unexpected aspects of the SUT through human powers of observation. Checking does not include the unexpected or unanticipated observations, so checking is limited to automation.

See automated checking.

See automated verifications.

See check.

See quality automation.

Cluster

See Verification Cluster.

Combined Engineering

Combined Engineering is a modern software development practice where developers also write the "test automation" or, in the context of this book, quality automation.

Deserialize

To create an object or data structure that can be used for software operations, from stored data or received stream.

Discoverability

An aspect of an application that allows a person who is not familiar with that application to discover how to use and get value from it according to the application design, without help from outside the application functionality, e.g., online help, a tutor, a book, or a manual.

End-to-End

A test that measures the application over the flow of a scenario from the point of view of an end-user is an end-to-end test. Typically, this would be a manual test.

Exploratory Testing

Testing independent of or in addition to a set of instructions or script, where a person notices and attempts un-scripted details.

False Negative

If a check passes, there is no alert; it is a negative event. If at some future point it becomes clear that the check should have failed, the negative is therefore false.

False Positive

A check failure that is not actionable is a false positive: a positive alert signal (fail), but false (not actionable).

This is also called a false test alarm, or false alarm.

Functional Requirement

A functional requirement is some required, measurable behavior of the SUT. Functional requirements connect to Business Requirements.

See Business Requirement.

Graphical User Interface

The interface of a software product intended for a human user, e.g., a web page as shown in a browser or the graphical touch screen of a mobile app.

GUI

See Graphical User Interface.

Harness

A tool for easy and efficient driving of automation code and collecting results.

Internet of Things

A network of assorted physical objects with widely varying purposes, where all have internet capability, either directly or through intermediary devices.

IoT

See Internet of Things.

Log

An element or elements of output from a process, based on isolated event or events in the process. The persisted log entry has a time stamp and any other information that was given for that event.

See Artifact.

Manual Testing

With manual, or human-guided testing, it is a person that decides whether some observed aspect of or issue with the SUT should be recorded and/or promoted as an action item or bug (whether or not the person is using any tools, aside from the SUT itself).

Contrast with Automated Checking.

MetaAutomation

MetaAutomation is a pattern language that shows a platform- and language-independent way of implementing optimal systems for the quality automation problem space. MetaAutomation provides stronger, more trustworthy, and detailed quality measurements. It enables better communication and collaboration, towards the goal of shipping higher-quality software faster and with happier teams.

See Quality Automation.

Pattern

For the context of this book, a pattern is a repeating solution to a problem in a context. A pattern is both language- and platform-independent.

The pattern concept is a useful tool to describing generalized solutions to problems.

See Pattern Language.

Pattern Language

A pattern language is a set of patterns that relate to each other with ordered dependencies.

For the context of this book, the pattern language MetaAutomation provides a solution to the quality automation problem space.

See Pattern.

See Quality Automation.

QA

See Quality Assurance.

Quality

Quality in the general sense is the value of the product to the customer or end-user. That value includes perceived qualities (e.g., correctness or usefulness) and qualities which might not be perceived (e.g., security, product behavior under stress, forward compatibility, etc.).

Quality is a very open-ended topic, and therefore challenging to encompass. This book focuses on functional correctness and performance quality.

See Quality Risk.

Quality Assurance

Quality assurance is the role that assures quality in the SUT, including functional quality.

Quality Automation

Quality automation is automation to support functional and performance quality as part of the software development process. The scope of quality automation includes:

- driving the SUT for quality measurements
- making those measurements
- recording the procedure and measurements
- improving business value of the quality data
- making both directed (i.e., push) and queryable (i.e., pull) communications of that data to the software business

Note that quality automation does not necessarily influence the style, contents, design, or language of product code.

The customers of quality automation include both people doing the software business, including developers, and automated processes, e.g., for continuous deployment of software.

Quality automation is the best method for measuring and communicating quality to the business, to answer these two questions:

1. Does the system do what we need it to do, for functional and performance quality measures?
2. By those measures of the first question, is quality for the SUT always getting better (or at least measurably the same), down to the control and granularity of individual code change submissions?

Quality automation code has no direct impact on end-users of the SUT, so coding styles and standards can have significant differences from product code.

See also Automated Checking.

Quality Portal

An intranet site for viewing and managing product quality, from data including check run artifacts, notification configuration and events, etc.

Quality Risk

This is the business risk from several potential sources:

- Quality issues impact team productivity
- Poor confidence in quality delays product ship
- Poor quality impacts company reputation
- Poor quality affects company valuation
- The product will not meet customers' needs sufficiently, for any reason

See Quality.

Regressing

Checking or testing to ensure that the correct and measured behaviors of the product continue to behave correctly.

Checking or testing to ensure that fixed bugs are still fixed.

Regression

Regression is shorthand for regression testing or checking.

See Regression Checking.

Regression Checking

Regressing checking focuses on verifying what is expected to be correct behavior of the SUT. Automated regression checking is very important to measure quality of the SUT and minimize the business risk that comes from uncertainty or lack of progress around the quality of the product, and in particular, minimizing the risk of impacting the entire product team with the negative effects of a significant break, i.e., a regression, in behavior of the SUT.

Regression also can include tests specifically focused on bugs that have been fixed, to ensure that the SUT continues to show the correct behavior. This is a useful technique because bugs tend to occur in higher-risk areas of product functionality, as bugs have a significant chance of re-occurring after they are fixed.

Regression Testing

In the context of automated checking, see Regression Checking.

In the context of manual testing, this is manual testing to ensure that system or functional requirements are still met, especially for those functional requirements that are too expensive to automate and sustain the automation.

Risk

Risk is that which degrades or interferes with predictability, so it is a cost to business.

See Quality Risk.

Root Cause

The root cause of a check failure, from a product developer's perspective, is the least-dependent contributing factor in product code owned by the team, or a combination of such factors or in combination with some issue with a dependent external service.

Scale

(verb) To increase in capability in direct proportion to input resources. For software, this means doing more of whatever the product does and faster with more processing power, machines or virtual machines.

(noun) The ability to scale.

SDLC

See Software Development Lifecycle.

Serialize

For software, to serialize an entity is to enable it to be stored or communicated as a linear stream of information.

See Deserialize.

SUT

See System under Test.

System Under Test (SUT), or System

The system under test (or, system for short) includes product code owned by the team developing the software. It excludes dependencies that are outside team ownership, and non-shipping code. Product code is code that will touch or impact end-users and any external dependent software systems.

Target Verification

A target verification characterizes the check. The focus of the check is expressed in the target verification, which includes one or more assertions of product behavior.

The target verification verifies correct product behavior.

See Verification.

See Verification Cluster.

Testing in Production

Testing in production runs the live – in production – product with automation and resources (accounts, identities, etc.)

specific to product quality efforts. This is done in a way that it does not impact end-users, at least not significantly, but it verifies correct behaviors for the system in production.

TIP

See Testing in Production.

Triage

In software development, triage is the process of examining, prioritizing, and delegating issues so that bugs or other action items keep moving around the team. For the scope of this book, triage involves following up on the artifacts of checks, whether manually or aided by automated processes, e.g., the Automated Triage pattern. The term "triage" derives from emergency medicine.

Unit Test

A verification or verifications that address a code deployment unit, i.e., an executable with a single file image, e.g., a lib or assembly.

In the scope of this book "unit test" refers to testing a unit.

See Test.

Verification

In software quality, verification is a measurement of whether the SUT meets a functional requirement. This is like a "test" but specifically focused on predetermined success criteria that automation can measure.

See Target Verification.

See Verification Cluster.

Verification Cluster

A group or cluster of more than one verification. This is a useful optimization for cases where more than one related functional requirement can be verified with no intervening interaction with executable code of the SUT. For example, on a single static web page, verifications of several required properties of similar priority would fit in a verification cluster. The result of a verification cluster is a Boolean pass/fail, with information on each verification in the cluster. A failure in a verification cluster never blocks any of the measurements in the cluster.

See Target Verification.

See Verification.

Notes

Agile Manifesto, Principles behind the, http://www.agilemanifesto.org/principles.html, retrieved 8/10/2018.

Alexander et al., *A Pattern Language: Towns, Buildings, Construction*, Oxford University Press (New York), 1977.

Alexander, Christopher, *A Timeless Way of Building*, Oxford University Press (New York), 1979.

Asimov, Isaac, "Intelligences Together," from *The Dangers of Intelligence and Other Science Essays*, 1986.

Association of Computing Machinery (ACM), draft 2 of "Code of Ethics," https://ethics.acm.org/2018-code-draft-2, 2018.

Beck, Kent, *Extreme Programming Explained*, Addison-Wesley, 2000.

Beizer, Boris, *Software Testing Techniques*, Van Nostrand Reinhold (New York), 1990.

Biddle, Robert, Carleton University Ottawa, from personal email 12/11/2017.

Binder, Robert V., *Testing Object-Oriented Systems: Models, Patterns and Tools*, Addison-Wesley, 2000.

Booch, Rumbaugh, and Jacobson, *The Unified Modeling Language User Guide*, Addison-Wesley, 1999.

Caspar, Mirko, Lippmann, Mirko, Hardt, Wolfram, "Automated system testing using dynamic and resource restricted clients," *Proceedings of the conference on Design, Automation & Test in Europe*, Article No. 322, March 2014.

Cessna, 1967 Model 172 And Skyhawk *Owner's Manual*, version copyright 1984.

Collins, Eliane Figueiredo, de Lucena, Jr., Vicente Ferreira, "Software test automation practices in agile development environment: an industry experience report," *Proceedings of the 7th International Workshop on Automation of Software Test*, p. 62, June 2012.

Coplien, James, "Seque," https://rbcs-us.com/documents/Segue.pdf, p. 10, retrieved 8/10/2018.

Coplien, James, "Why Most Unit Testing is Waste," http://www.rbcs-us.com/documents/Why-Most-Unit-Testing-is-Waste.pdf, p. 10, 2014.

Davies, Steven, Roper, Marc, "What's in a bug report?" *Proceedings of the 8th ACM/IEEE International Symposium on Empirical Software Engineering and Measurement*, p. 2, September 2014.

Elbaum, Sebastian, Rothermel, Gregg, Penix, John, "Techniques for improving regression testing in continuous integration development environments," *Proceedings of the 22nd ACM SIGSOFT International Symposium on Foundations of Software Engineering*, p. 235, November 2014.

Evans, Eric, *Domain-Driven Design: Tackling Complexity in the Heart of Software*, Addison-Wesley, 2003.

Farias, Giovanni et al., "Distributed test agents: a pattern for the development of automatic system tests for distributed applications," *Proceedings of the 9th Latin-American Conference on Pattern Languages of Programming*, September 2012.

Fowler and Scott, *UML Distilled Second Edition*, Addison-Wesley, 2000.

Fowler, "StranglerApplication" https://www.martinfowler.com/bliki/StranglerApplication.html, retrieved 8/10/2018, 2004.

Gabriel, Richard P., *Patterns of Software: Tales from the Software Community*, Oxford University Press, 1996.

Gamma et al, *Design Patterns*, Addison-Wesley, p. 163, 1995.

Garg & Sharapov, *Techniques for Optimizing Applications - High Performance Computing*, Prentice-Hall, 2002.

Garg, Deepak, Datta, Amitava, "Parallel execution of prioritized test cases for regression testing of web applications," *Proceedings of the Thirty-Sixth Australasian Computer Science Conference* - Volume 135, February 2013.

Gerrard, Paul, "Digital Transformation, Testing and Automation," webinar 2/5/2016a.

Gerrard, Paul, from email discussion, 9/12/2016b.

Gierloff, Jana, "From Quality Control to Quality Assistance," presentation at STPCon Spring 2017.

Goldsmith, Robin F., *Discovering REAL Business Requirements for Software Project Success*, Artech House, 2004.

Goldsmith, Robin F., "Proactive SQA Overcomes Traditional 'Traffic Cop' SQA Resistance," *PNSQC 2016* conference, 2016.

Goucher, Adam, "Quality through Innovation," Retrieved June 1st, 2017 from http://adam.goucher.ca/?cat=3, 2008.

Graham, Dorothy and Fewster, Mark, *Experiences of Test Automation: Case Studies of Software Test Automation*, Addison-Wesley, 2012.

Grizzaffi, Paul, "Heresy II – Comments Are Code," https://responsibleautomation.wordpress.com/2018/02/01/heresy-ii-comments-are-code/, retrieved 8/10/2018, 2018.

Guerra, Eduardo et al., "Patterns for testing distributed systems interaction," *Proceedings of the 21st Conference on Pattern Languages of Programs*, September 2014.

Harrison, Neil B., "The Language of Shepherding," Hillside Group, http://hillside.net/documents/language-of-shepherding.pdf, p.16, retrieved 8/10/2018, 1999.

Hendrickson, Elisabeth, "Gathering Requirements in a Low-Process Environment," *Software Management & Applications of Software Measurement 2003 Conference*, San Jose, CA, June 2nd, 2003.

Hendrickson, Elisabeth, personal email, 2/8/2016.

Herzig, Kim, Nagappan, Nachiappan, "Empirically detecting false test alarms using association rules," *Proceedings of the 37th International Conference on Software Engineering* – Volume 2, p. 42, May 2015.

Hoffman, Douglas, personal communication, PNSQC 2011.

Huizinga, Dorota and Kolawa, Adam, "Automated Defect Prevention," John Wiley & Sons Inc., 2007.

Humble and Farley, "Continuous Delivery," Addison-Wesley, 2011.

International Software Testing Qualifications Board (ISTQB), Standard glossary of terms used in Software Testing: Version 2.2, 2012.

Jiang, He, Li, Xiaochen, Zijiang Yang, Jifeng Xuan, "What causes my test alarm?: automatic cause analysis for test alarms in system and integration testing," *Proceedings of the 39th International Conference on Software Engineering*, p. 712-714, May 2017.

Kappler, Sebastian, "Finding and breaking test dependencies to speed up test execution," *Proceedings of the 2016 24th ACM SIGSOFT International Symposium on Foundations of Software Engineering*, p. 1136, November 2016.

Koster, Ken, "Using Portfolio Theory for Better and More Consistent Quality," *Proceedings of the 2007 international symposium on Software testing and analysis*, Abstract, July 2007.

Kuhn, Thomas S., *The Structure of Scientific Revolutions*, The University of Chicago Press, 1962.

Leszak, Marek, Perry, Dewayne E., Stoll, Dieter, "A case study in root cause defect analysis," *Proceedings of the 22nd international conference on Software engineering*, June 2000.

Maslow, *The Psychology of Being*, Van Nostrand Reinhold, p. 15, 1968.

Meszaros, Gerard, "A Pattern Language for Pattern Writing," Hillside Group, http://hillside.net/index.php/a-pattern-language-for-pattern-writing, Retrieved 11/1/2017, 1997.

Meszaros, Gerard, *xUnit Test Patterns*, Addison-Wesley, 2007.

MSDN, "Retry Pattern," http://msdn.microsoft.com/en-us/library/dn589788.aspx, retrieved 8/1/2018, 2015.

Myers, Glenford J., *The Art of Software Testing*, John Wiley & Sons, 1979.

Neubauer, Johannes, et al., "Automated continuous quality assurance," *Proceedings of the First International Workshop on Formal Methods in Software Engineering: Rigorous and Agile Approaches*, p. 42, June 2012.

Page, Johnston, and Rollison, *How We Test Software at Microsoft*, Microsoft Press, 2009.

Page, Alan, "Adventures in Modern Testing" for QASIG, Seattle WA, talk given 1/10/2018.

Parveen, Tauhida, Tilley, Scott, Gonzalez, George, "A case study in test management," *ACM-SE 45 Proceedings of the 45th annual southeast regional conference*, p. 86, March 2007.

Port, Dan, et al., "What we have learned about the value of software assurance," *Proceedings of the 8th ACM/IEEE International Symposium on Empirical Software Engineering and Measurement*, p. 1, September 2014.

Riley & Goucher, "Beautiful Testing," O'Reilly Media, 2010.

Roseberry, Wayne, "Winning with Flaky Test Automation," *Proceedings of Pacific Northwest Software Quality Conference* (PNSQC), http://uploads.pnsqc.org/2016/papers/12.WinningWithFlakyTestAutomation.pdf, retrieved 8/10/2018, 2016.

Roseberry, Wayne, personal email, 2017.

Salingaros, Nikos A., "The Structure of Pattern Languages," http://zeta.math.utsa.edu/~yxk833/StructurePattern.html, introduction, retrieved 8/10/2018, 2000.

Sebillotte, Suzanne, "Hierarchical planning as method for task analysis: the example of office task analysis," *Behaviour & Information Technology*, 7:3, 275-293, DOI:10.1080/01449298808901878, 1988.

Shore, James and Warden, Shane, *The Art of Agile Development*, O'Reilly Media, 2008.

Srivastva, Praveen Ranjan, Kumar, Krishan, and Raghurama G, "Test Case Prioritization Based on Requirements and Risk Factors," *ACM SIGSOFT Software Engineering Notes* Archive Volume 33 Issue 4, p.1, July 2008.

Switzer, Lorne and Lin, Hui, "Corporate governance, compliance and valuation effects of Sarbanes-Oxley on US and foreign firms," *International Journal of Business Governance and Ethics* Vol. 4 No. 4, https://www.academia.edu/25755925/Corporate_governance_compliance_and_valuation_effects_of_Sarbanes-Oxley_on_US_and_foreign_firms, downloaded 8/10/2018, 2009.

Tomlinson, Mark, personal conversation at STPcon Spring 2017, 2017a.

Tomlinson, Mark, by Skype conference, 5/5/2017b.

Whittaker, James, *How Google Tests Software*, Addison-Wesley, 2012.

Wikipedia, "Pattern Language," https://en.wikipedia.org/wiki/Pattern_language, retrieved 8/10/2018.

Wikipedia, "Sarbanes-Oxley Act," https://en.wikipedia.org/wiki/Sarbanes–Oxley_Act, retrieved 8/10/2018.

Wilson, Edward O, *Consilience: The Unity of Knowledge*, Vintage Books, A Division of Random House, New York, p.14, 1998.

Index

example: experiments we cannot
  control, 128
example: performance criteria, 127–
  128
forces, 127
problem, 127
resulting context, 127
review questions, 128
solution, 127
summary, 125–126
external services, 65–66

F

false negative
  defined, 220
  fixing defect escape/false negative
    problem, 48
  lower rate due to MetaAutomation, 23
false positive
  defined, 220
  fixing, 47
  lower rate due to MetaAutomation, 23,
    25–26
Farias, Giovanni, 173
Farley, David, 33–34
feedback, faster, 22–23
fixing test automation. *See* test automation
flaky tests, 20
forces, patterns, 76
Four-Phase Test pattern, 133
functional requirement, defined, 220
future patterns, 159–160

G

Gabriel, Richard, 69
Gerrard, Paul, 30
Gierloff, Jana, 22
glossary, 10
glue code, 34–35
Goldsmith, Robin, 22, 29, 35, 78, 79, 80,
  81, 82, 108
Goucher, Adam, 99

Grizzaffi, Paul, 47
Guerra, Eduardo, 173
GUI (Graphical User Interface)
  benefits of MetaAutomation, 28
  defined, 221
  Event-Driven Check example, 123–
    124

H

harness, defined, 221
headless testing, 64–65
Hendrickson, Elisabeth, 79, 201
Herzig, Kim, 47–48, 87
Hierarchical Steps, 69, 74, 85–98
  context, 86
  example: the Composite pattern, 92
  example: BankingAds, 97–98
  example: business task, 93–95
  example: buying a plane ticket, 97
  example: cooking with a recipe, 93
  example: installing a dishwasher, 92–93
  example: preflight for a small airplane,
    95–96
  forces, 87–88
  naturalness of, 46–47
  problem, 87
  quantum leap, 69
  resulting context, 91–92
  review questions, 98
  solution, 88–91
  summary, 85–86
Hoffman, Douglas, 29
Huizinga, Dorota, 18, 102
Humble, Jez, 33–34

I

impact map, 191
implicit verification, Atomic Check, 103
Internet of things (IoT)
  benefits of MetaAutomation, 28
  defined, 221
  multiple tiers, 65

risk, defined, 223

root cause, defined, 224

Roper, Marc, 44

Roseberry, Wayne, 149, 154, 204

S

Salingaros, Nikos, 70

samples, 10

how to use samples, 163–166

review questions (How to Use the Samples), 166

Sample 1, 167–170

Sample 2, 171–172

Sample 3, 173–76

Sarbanes-Oxley (SOX), 20–21, 26, 158

scale, defined, 224

scaled check runs, 173

scripting languages, 197–199

existing automation, 196

Sebillotte, Suzanne, 93–94

sending notifications, 187–188

sequence diagrams

checks running sequentially, 138

example check set run, 181–182

Sample 3, 175

serialize, defined, 224

Setup and Teardown, Four-Phase Test, 133

shift left testing, benefits of MetaAutomation, 33

Smart Retry, 75, 141–150

configuring timeout for failure-prone checks, 147–148

context, 141–143

example: "Retry" pattern, 148–149

example: BankingAds, 149

example: web site with AJAX, 149–150

forces, 143

problem, 143

resulting context, 148

review questions, 150

solution, 143–148

summary, 141–142

software development, unifying with quality automation, 5–6

software teams

faster feedback, 22–23

improved communication, 23

low false negative rate, 23

solutions, patterns, 76

SOX (Sarbanes-Oxley), 20–21, 26, 158

Srivastva, Praveen Ranjan, 108

summaries, patterns, 76

SUT (System Under Test)

defined, 224

recording all that is going on, 44

synthetics, benefits of MetaAutomation, 28

system tests, 203

T

target verification

Atomic Check, 104

defined, 224

Made in the USA
Monee, IL
21 September 2021